The Habsburgs

An Enthralling Overview of One of The Most Important Dynasties in European History

Free limited time bonus

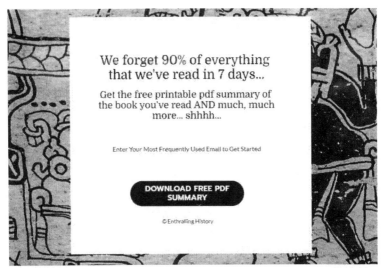

Stop for a moment. We have a free bonus set up for you. The problem is this: we forget 90% of everything that we read after 7 days. Crazy fact, right? Here's the solution: we've created a printable, 1-page pdf summary for this book that you're reading now. All you have to do to get your free pdf summary is to go to the following website: https://livetolearn.lpages.co/enthrallinghistory/

Or, Scan the QR code!

Once you do, it will be intuitive. Enjoy, and thank you!

Table of Contents

INTRODUCTION 1

CHAPTER 1: THE HOUSE OF HABSBURG RISES.............................3

CHAPTER 2: THE ROYAL MARRIAGES.....................................10

CHAPTER 3: CHARLES AND THE GLOBAL HABSBURG EMPIRE 17

CHAPTER 4: THE WEALTH OF THE NEW WORLD..........................29

CHAPTER 5: THE OTTOMAN-HABSBURG WAR 38

CHAPTER 6: ARTS, SCIENCES, AND HABSBURG PATRONAGE.............46

CHAPTER 7: RELIGIOUS TENSIONS AND THE THIRTY YEARS' WAR....60

CHAPTER 8: THE SPANISH SUCCESSION 72

CHAPTER 9: THE REIGN OF MARIA THERESA 83

CHAPTER 10: THE NAPOLEONIC ERA AND THE AGE OF
METTERNICH..92

CHAPTER 11: THE DUAL MONARCHY......................................103

CHAPTER 12: THE END OF THE HABSBURG DYNASTY 112

CONCLUSION 121

HERE'S ANOTHER BOOK BY ENTHRALLING HISTORY THAT
YOU MIGHT LIKE...123

FREE LIMITED TIME BONUS...124

BIBLIOGRAPHY 125

Introduction

The history of Europe is intertwined with the story of the Habsburgs, one of the oldest and most powerful families in Europe for centuries. Originating from the Austrian territories of Tyrol in the late medieval period, the Habsburg dynasty quickly expanded its reach across central and eastern Europe, eventually becoming the most significant political dynasty on the continent. Throughout their long reigns, the Habsburgs faced numerous challenges, yet they persisted and became one of the most significant and influential dynasties in European history.

The Habsburg dynasty came to power at a time when Europe was undergoing massive transformations. The 15th and 16th centuries, in particular, were characterized by religious, political, and social upheaval. It was during this period that the Habsburgs rose to imperial power, bolstering their position through marriages and military conquests. Their most significant triumph was the acquisition of the Duchy of Burgundy in 1477, which gave them access to resources that they used to expand their power base.

In the mid-16th century, the Habsburgs established one of the most significant territorial empires in Europe. Their provinces included the Spanish Empire, Austria, Hungary, and various territories in the Balkans. The Habsburg Empire became a dominant force in Europe thanks to its vast resources, talented leadership, and military might. The Habsburgs waged wars against the Ottoman Turks, which helped to preserve Christianity in Europe. They also engaged in political alliances that helped them to maintain their position.

However, like all dynasties, the Habsburgs faced significant challenges. One of their most significant adversaries was the Reformation movement, which was gaining ground in Europe during the 16th and 17th centuries. The Habsburgs, being devout Catholics, tried to stamp out the movement, which led to a series of religious wars across Europe. The Thirty Years' War, which started in 1618, saw the Habsburgs fighting against various Protestant states and almost led to the demise of their dynasty. However, the war ended in 1648 with the signing of the Treaty of Westphalia, which marked the end of major religious wars in Europe and saw the Habsburgs maintain their position.

The Habsburgs faced another significant challenge in the 18th and 19th centuries, as they lost territories to rising powers such as Prussia and France. The loss of their power base significantly weakened the dynasty, and it eventually collapsed in 1918 following the First World War.

Despite this, the impact of the Habsburgs on Europe remains significant to this day, making them one of the most significant and notable dynasties in European history.

Chapter 1: The House of Habsburg Rises

It all started in the Alps. The road that led the Habsburgs to the heights of incredible glory and power began in the Swiss canton of Aargau. The dynasty's founding father is Guntram the Rich, who lived in the 10th century. The dynastic momentum started to build in the 11th century.

The European political landscape at that time was a tapestry of feudal kingdoms and principalities. The Habsburgs were a part of it, and they were not the most notable family. Nevertheless, they flourished and grew as other noble families died out. Radbot of Klettgau is a noteworthy member of the family's early history because he built Habsburg Castle in the early 11th century.[1]

The Habsburgs' holdings were modest at the beginning. Other families, such as the Hohenstaufen noble family, held more power and influence. Yet, the Habsburgs developed a strategy that served them well in the years to come. It was marriage.

The sacrament of matrimony was not a festival of love in those days. Instead, it was a means by which families would enter into strategic alliances, and dowries could be gifts of land. Territorial acquisitions increased the size of the Habsburgs' domain so that by the 13th century,

---

[1] The World of the Habsburgs. (2023, October 21). The Habsburgs' Origins as a Swiss Noble Family. Retrieved from The World of the Habsburgs:
https://www.habsburger.net/en/chapter/habsburgs-origins-swiss-noble-family.

they were the most important family between the Upper Rhine and the Alps. The family was ready for a great leap forward. That happened in 1273.

In that year, Rudolf Habsburg was elected the king of the Romans and Germany. This election was no doubt a compromise among the empire's electors, who were looking for stability after the collapse of the Hohenstaufen dynasty. Rudolf was a very shrewd and astute politician. In the words of Otto of Freising, "Through his wit and God's grace, Rudolf rose from the shadows, and all were awed by his ascent."[2]

Rudolf was no longer a poor count but the most powerful man in central Europe.[3]

Gaining Respectability

Rudolf was aware that he had to move quickly and decisively to cement his control. King Ottokar of Bohemia was his biggest rival. Ottokar opposed Rudolf's election, and Rudolf reciprocated by declaring Ottokar's land forfeit. In the Battle of Marchfeld in 1278, Rudolf won a victory, and Ottokar was killed in the fight.

Rudolf capitalized on this by claiming Austria and Styria. He then gifted the territories to his sons Albert and Rudolf, giving the Habsburgs a land base that would be in the family's hands for centuries.

Rudolf used marriage as a means of diplomacy. He married his daughter Judith to Wenceslaus of Bohemia, which permitted him to neutralize a possible threat while forging an alliance with a very powerful neighbor.

Rudolf would continue to work on gaining positive recognition. He followed policies that favored the Roman Catholic Church and reestablished imperial authority in German regions that had grown too independent. He used political and military maneuvering to make his family the preeminent noble house in Germany.

Adolf of Nassau succeeded Rudolf because the electors were concerned about the dynastic aspirations of the Habsburgs and did not

---

[2] The World of the Habsburgs. (2023, October 21). Rudolf I of Habsburgs: From "Poor Count" to King of the Romans. Retrieved from The World of the Habsburgs: https://www.habsburger.net/en/chapter/rudolf-i-habsburg-poor-count-king-romans.

[3] The World of the Habsburgs. (2023, October 21). Rudolf I of Habsburgs: From "Poor Count" to King of the Romans. Retrieved from The World of the Habsburgs: https://www.habsburger.net/en/chapter/rudolf-i-habsburg-poor-count-king-romans.

want a hereditary monarchy. Adolf was unpopular, though, and was killed in the Battle of Göllheim. He was then succeeded by Rudolf's son Albert, who was elected the German king on July 27th, 1298.

Albert I

Albert Habsburg was a very intelligent man and continued his father's legacy of astute statesmanship. He had a firm understanding of the politics of the time. Albert would use military force if he had to, but he mainly relied on his ability to govern.

Albert had a well-rounded education that gave him a broad worldview and allowed him to approach governing with a combination of pragmatism and innovation. He was a reader and was intellectually curious. Albert maintained close ties with scholars and fostered the development of the University of Vienna. His intellectual talents helped him enormously in the areas of diplomacy.

King Albert I recognized how fractional disputes destabilized central Europe. Consequently, he worked to centralize administrative functions, and he promoted legal justice. His understanding of Roman canon law helped him initiate necessary legal reforms.

Albert was an interesting figure. His sense of justice was not limited to how much he might benefit from it. He offered protection to the Jews, and serfs found a friend in this stern man. He understood the importance of cities and how these urban centers were good for the economy. Albert gave privileges to various cities, and these concessions enabled them to become trade hubs. However, Albert was assassinated in 1308 by his nephew, who had been denied his right of inheritance by Albert.

King Albert I.

The 14th century was a crucial time for the Habsburgs in regard to their future trajectory in European politics. The principal Habsburgs were Duke Frederick I of Austria and Leopold I, who was the co-ruler of Austria with his brother.

The family used its time to consolidate its power and increase its territory. Bohemia was a strategic target that would enhance Habsburg influence in central Europe. After an attempt to seize the crown of Bohemia failed, the Habsburgs turned their attention to the south, where they were very successful. In 1311, they secured Savinja in modern-day Slovenia. Next, they took control of Carniola and Carinthia in 1335 and then took the Tyrol in 1369. Additional territories in the following years included Pazia (1374) and Trieste (1382). What is noteworthy about these acquisitions is that they were not taken in battle but after the death of the existing rulers.

They did pay a price for their successes. The original home territories of the Habsburgs in Switzerland, including Habsburg Castle, were swallowed up by the Swiss Confederacy. By the end of the 14th century, the Habsburgs' land was primarily in what is now modern Austria. Numerous members of the family held royal titles in central Europe, including Frederick III (King of Germany, r. 1314-1330) and Albert V (Duke of Austria, r. 1404-1439; King of Hungary and Croatia, r. 1437-1439; King of the Romans as Albert II, r. 1438-1439; and King of Bohemia, r. 1438-1439).

Albert II

Albert II's life is remarkable since his marriage put him in a position to gain titles without having to lead armies. He became king of Hungary and Bohemia because he was the husband to the daughter and heiress of Sigismund, who was king of both countries. Although Albert was pronounced king of the Romans, he was never crowned Holy Roman emperor.

Albert II, King of the Romans.
https://commons.wikimedia.org/wiki/File:Albrecht_II_as_Roman-German_king.jpg

Albert II was also known for his harassment of the Jews. He established new taxes on the Jewish community to finance military campaigns and accused them of collaborating with his enemies. Albert used the accusation of Jews desecrating the Host in 1420 to finally destroy the Jewish community in Austria.

Albert used the accusation to force Jews to either convert or face imprisonment. Jews were deported and tortured. The forced baptism of Jewish children was stopped only by the intervention of Pope Martin V. Albert's final act of persecution happened on March 12th, 1421. Ninety-two men and 120 women were burned at the stake south of the city walls of Vienna. Jews were then placed under an eternal ban, and their synagogue was demolished.

Albert II was succeeded by his son, Ladislaus. He is known to history as Ladislaus the Posthumous because he was born a few months after his father's death. The passing of Albert II allowed Ladislaus to become duke of Austria and the king of Hungary, Croatia, and eventually Bohemia. Ladislaus died in 1457 when he was only seventeen years old. His death caused the Habsburg territories to be divided.

Frederick III

There was another Habsburg on the scene at this time. Frederick became the duke of Styria, Carinthia, and Carniola in 1424 when he was nine years old. He became a principal player in European history when he was elected and crowned the king of Germany in 1440. Frederick was formally crowned Holy Roman emperor in 1452. He was the longest-reigning Holy Roman emperor, holding the title for fifty-three years.

Frederick was not a great military man and was criticized by some historians for being too passive. However, he achieved his objectives without spilling a lot of blood. Frederick was patient and was able to sit out various political situations. He was more of a diplomat and strategic thinker. Frederick triumphed in certain situations simply because he outlived his opponents and inherited their land. He also used dynastic marriage as a means of achieving goals. His most significant success was to compel Charles the Bold of Burgundy to give his daughter, Mary of Burgundy, to his son Maximilian.

Frederick had a personal motto, "A.E.I.O.U.," which was imprinted on all his belongings. He never explained to anybody what it meant, but historians have suggested that it stood for "Alles Erdreich ist Österreich Untertan" ("All the world is subject to Austria").[4]

---

[4] Holy Roman Empire Association. (2023, October 21). Holy Roman Emperor Frederick III-1440-1493. Retrieved from Holy Roman Empire Association: http://www.holyromanempireassociation.com/holy-roman-emperor-frederick-iii-.html.

Frederick and Maximilian ruled jointly for the last ten years of Frederick's life. He died in 1493 and was succeeded by Maximilian.

Maximilian's succession was a significant turning point in the history of the Habsburg family. They were no longer regional aristocrats or insignificant monarchs. The twenty-six years following Frederick's death would see the Habsburgs vault over the Tudor and Valois families to become the primary dynastic family of Europe.

The years to come were heady for the family that had started in Switzerland and gradually moved to the imperial court. As the century progressed, the Habsburgs' prestige and power grew. Their territories sprawled, their coffers swelled, and their influence began to reverberate throughout the European courts. Such was the clout they wielded that when Charles IV, Holy Roman Emperor, needed allies, he turned to the Habsburgs, sealing the pact with the marriage of his daughter to Albert II.

It is evident that the foundations of the Habsburg dynasty were intricately laid with a blend of ambition, shrewd alliances, and fortuitous events. With Austria and surrounding territories firmly under their control, the stage was set for a dynamic future. The consolidation of Habsburg power, which had been carefully and methodically achieved, laid the groundwork for the dynasty's future successes and their pivotal role in shaping history. Next, we will delve deeper into the labyrinth of Habsburg power, exploring how the family's foundational strength paved the way for an empire on which the sun never set.

Chapter 2: The Royal Marriages

Marrying for love is a romantic notion that gained popularity in the Victorian era. It was more of a business decision before that time; a couple got married and hopefully discovered love later on. Marriage was a sacrament in the church, but it was also a contract and a diplomatic tool in the eyes of the 15th-century aristocracy.

In the medieval and early modern periods of European history, matrimony was not just a personal matter but was pivotal to the political, territorial, and diplomatic strategies of dynasties. Among the intricate tapestry of European royals, few played the matrimonial game as adeptly as the Habsburgs.

Understanding the Sacrament/Contract

Before delving into the Habsburgs, it is crucial to understand the broader European tradition of marriage as a political tool. During the medieval and early modern eras, royal weddings aimed to secure political alliances, end hostilities, or guarantee inheritances. Unlike today, these unions were rarely about love; instead, they served as strategic instruments wielded by ruling families to cement their influence and expand territories.

Territory and lineage were deeply interwoven, and feudal practices and customs reinforced this pattern. Powerful lords, for instance, might marry off their daughters to secure an alliance or a vassal's loyalty. For monarchs, the stakes were even higher. A suitable marriage could mean the acquisition of entire kingdoms or critical buffer zones.

The status of a marriage could also spell the difference between peace in the land or civil war. For instance, the validity of a royal wedding and the children produced played a significant role in the Wars of the Roses and the eventual success of the Tudor family.

There were several critical dynastic marriages in the 15th century:

- John II of Aragon and Juana Enríquez (1444)

This union was significant in consolidating the Trastámara dynasty's rule in Aragon. Their son, Ferdinand II, would go on to marry Isabella I of Castile, marking the beginning of a united Spain.

- Ferdinand II of Aragon and Isabella I of Castile (1469)

Known as the "Catholic Monarchs," their union effectively unified Spain. Together, they completed the Reconquista, expelling the Muslims from Granada, sponsored Christopher Columbus's 1492 voyage, and initiated the Spanish Inquisition.

- Richard III of England and Anne Neville (1472)

This marriage closely tied Richard to the Warwick inheritance and the northern estates. It consolidated his power and further complicated the intricate family and political dynamics of the Wars of the Roses.

- Henry VII of England and Elizabeth of York (1486)

This marriage united the warring houses of Lancaster and York, symbolically ending the Wars of the Roses. It laid the foundation for the Tudor dynasty, with their son, Henry VIII, and granddaughter, Elizabeth I, becoming two of the most notable monarchs in English history.

These marriages demonstrate the intricate interplay of power dynamics, alliances, and territorial ambitions in 15th-century Europe. Let's take a look at how the Habsburgs utilized political marriages to their advantage.

The Burgundian Union

The Burgundian union was arguably the most significant marriage of the century, and it underscores the genius of the Habsburg matrimonial strategy. The marriage of Frederick III's son, Maximilian I of Austria, to Mary of Burgundy epitomizes how marriages were leveraged to secure vast swathes of land and power. It was a drama with incredible consequences.

The opening scene of this high-energy play is on a battlefield near the city of Nancy in Lorraine. Charles the Bold, Duke of Burgundy, was engaged in a campaign to take the Duchy of Savoy, and things were not going well for him. Against the advice of his generals, Charles led a small force against a larger army on January 5th, 1477, and was routed. The duke's frozen corpse was found in a pool of water on January 7th.[5]

In the 15th century, the Burgundian territories represented a significant portion of western Europe, comprising much of present-day eastern France, Belgium, and parts of the Netherlands. Economically, the Burgundian state was one of Europe's wealthiest due to its robust textile industry, trade routes, and the bustling cities of Ghent, Bruges, and Antwerp. Moreover, the geopolitical location of Burgundy as a buffer between France and the Holy Roman Empire magnified its strategic importance.

Mary of Burgundy was Europe's most sought-after bride, as she was the sole heir to Charles the Bold, Duke of Burgundy. Her inheritance included the Burgundian Netherlands, a patchwork of territories stretching from modern-day France to the Netherlands. With Charles's unexpected death in 1477, Mary became a key figure in European politics. Recognizing the immense geopolitical ramifications of controlling Burgundy, Louis XI of France sought to annex parts of the duchy and, if possible, align Mary with a French prince.

Frederick III, Holy Roman Emperor and Maximilian's father, was acutely aware of the value of a Burgundian alliance. In a Europe dominated by matrimonial politics, securing Mary's hand for Maximilian was both a defensive and an offensive move. There had been earlier attempts to broker a marriage in 1473 that failed. Mary, who was now the duchess of Burgundy, was worried about the intentions of Louis XI to absorb Burgundy and reopened marriage negotiations with Frederick III.[6]

Frederick III moved quickly to bring the negotiations to a successful conclusion. The emperor promptly dispatched envoys to negotiate with Mary and her advisors. Frederick signaled a willingness to provide military support to protect Mary against possible French aggression. He

[5] Abernethy, S. (2013, May 3). Charles the Bold, Duke of Burgundy. Retrieved from The Freelance History Writer: https://thefreelancehistorywriter.com/2013/05/03/charles-the-bold-duke-of-burgundy/.
[6] Flantzer, S. (2023, May 29). Mary, Duchess of Burgundy, Archduchess of Austria. Retrieved from Unofficial Royalty: https://www.unofficialroyalty.com/mary-duchess-of-burgundy-archduchess-of-austria/.

also helped financially to make all the negotiations successful. Frederick was not wealthy and had to secure a loan to pay for all the expenses. He, therefore, approached the most influential financiers of the time.

Understanding Renaissance Loan Management

Marriage alliances required a substantial amount of money right away. Monarchs could not wait for taxes to be collected; if they waited, someone with the available funds could make an offer. The finances of Renaissance banking could be the topic of a whole book, but it is worthwhile to know how bankers moved the money into the hands of debtors.

The Renaissance witnessed a surge in the need for credit and financial services to fund dynamic economic expansion. The Roman Catholic Church created an obstacle: the practice of usury. The church condemned charging any amount of interest on loans.

This prohibition stems from Thomas Aquinas's opinions on usury. This Doctor of the Church argued that money was a sterile medium and could not by itself breed money, making interest on loans unnatural. According to Aquinas, money was created for the purpose of exchange, not to increase wealth through charged interest. Earnings did not come from economic activity but from the money itself. And that, in the opinion of Aquinas, was morally reprehensible.

Aquinas believed that people who took out loans were people who really needed money to take care of themselves and their families. The lender did not need the money since he had the necessary resources to cover the loan. If they charged interest, then they would be taking advantage of those in need.[7]

He was not the only one who thought that usury was wrong. In the *Divine Comedy*, Dante places those who practice usury in a particular part of hell. They are in the seventh circle and are condemned for a form of violence that is against both natural and moral order. Dante has usurers roasting in hell with heavy purses hung around their necks.

Bankers had to find a way to justify what they were doing, and they used several means. The *contractum trinius* was a way of going around

---

[7] Munoz, J. A. (2019, September 20). Profit vs. Usury: Difference from the Point of View of Saint Thomas Aquinas. Retrieved from The Tseconomist: https://thetseconomist.wordpress.com/2019/09/20/profit-vs-usury-difference-from-the-point-of-view-of-saint-thomas-aquinas/.

the usury laws. The *contractum trinius* was a set of three contracts: an investment, a profit sale, and an insurance contract. These were offered to those seeking a loan.

The lending banker would invest an amount equal to the financing needed by the borrower for a year. The lender would then purchase insurance on the investment from the borrower and sell the borrower the right to any profit made over a prearranged percentage from the investment. The lender was protected from default, and the law protected the borrower from any attempt to collect money by force.

Rent charges and bills of exchange were also used to charge interest without actually charging interest. There would come a day when the Catholic Church withdrew its opposition to interest, and monarchs who were in need of money protected the bankers.

When considering the financial world of the Renaissance, the Medici family of Florence often comes to mind first. They were the bankers of popes and great patrons of the arts. Nevertheless, there was another banking dynasty that was arguably just as powerful as the House of Medici. This other family was the Fuggers, and they were headquartered in Augsburg. Both families were willing to work with the Holy Roman emperor.

Significant financial resources were required to ensure the marriage between Maximilian and Mary. We do not have comprehensive records of the exact terms of the loans made to Frederick. This is probably due to the complex arrangements and agreements that were sometimes verbal and had non-standardized contracts. The loans from the Medici family typically involved high-interest rates for sovereigns. Collateral in the form of revenue from taxes, customs duties, or possibly territorial holdings was what the Medici wanted in return for their cash.

The Fuggers were known for securing trade privileges, mining rights, or other concessions in return for their financial services. Both banking houses were known to drive hard bargains, and Frederick had to be willing to deal.

Bankers had a good reason to be firm. Loaning money to a monarch was very risky. Edward III of England defaulted on his debts to the Badi and Peruzzi banking houses of Florence, causing both to collapse. A ruler's death could cause a succession crisis, which might result in policy changes that would increase financial risk to a lender. In addition, there was no clear legal framework for international lending and debt enforcement. Bankers were vulnerable to defaults.

Cost-benefit analysis indicates that whatever Frederick had to promise, it had to be worth it. After all, the Habsburgs would have a connection with Burgundy that would strengthen the family's position against France and expand Habsburg territory. The economic vitality of Burgundy would add tremendous value to the Habsburg name. Burgundy proved to be a major asset.

A Power Couple

Frederick III's diplomacy and political efforts ultimately succeeded. Maximilian and Mary were married in Ghent on August 19th, 1477. The nuptials had immediate and profound implications.

- Halting French expansion: Louis XI was able to annex Burgundy and other Burgundian territories, but with the marriage, French aspirations for additional annexation were thwarted.
- Territorial acquisitions for the Habsburgs: The marriage paved the way for the Habsburgs to lay claim to the vast Burgundian territories, including what is modern-day Belgium, the Netherlands, and Luxembourg, significantly enhancing their stature in Europe.
- Tensions with France: The union sowed the seeds for heightened tensions and future conflicts between the Habsburgs and the Valois and later Bourbon monarchs of France. Habsburg possessions were now pressing on French borders, and land disputes would surface constantly during the next few centuries.

The marriage was a foundational moment in the rise of the Habsburg dynasty as a dominant European power. Their descendants would go on to control vast territories across Europe and even claim the Spanish throne.

The union also shifted the balance of power in Europe, setting the stage for centuries of conflicts, alliances, and rivalries, particularly involving the French and the Habsburgs. It would be nearly three hundred years before France and the Habsburg Empire ceased being bitter enemies.

Contemporary records paint Maximilian as a dynamic and savvy politician. Similarly, Mary's character emerged from the pages of history as both steadfast and politically astute.

Best of all, the marriage was a love match. Maximilian and Mary were devoted to each other. Their correspondence hints at a partnership based on mutual respect, a rarity in politically arranged marriages.

The Maximilian-Mary union bore fruit both literally and politically. Their offspring, Philip the Handsome and Margaret of Austria, would go on to make their own pivotal matrimonial alliances. Philip married Joanna of Castile, leading to the Habsburgs inheriting Spain and its vast colonial empire.

The Habsburgs' marital strategy undoubtedly shaped the map of Europe. Their dynasty, at its zenith, controlled Spain, Austria, parts of Germany, the Low Countries, and vast colonial territories. However, this strategy also sowed the seeds of their decline. The intricate web of alliances and intermarriages led to genetic complications (most notably, the Habsburg jaw) and intricate political quagmires.

The intertwining of so many royal houses meant that succession issues frequently arose. By marrying within a limited pool of royal families (sometimes resorting to intermarriage within their own family), the Habsburgs occasionally faced challenges and even wars of succession.

Nonetheless, their strategy also provided stability, fostering a period of artistic and scientific revival in territories under their rule.

The Habsburgs exemplified the potential and the pitfalls of using marriage as a tool of geopolitical strategy. Their rise to power through marital alliances underscores the importance of matrimony in medieval and early modern Europe. At the same time, their eventual challenges serve as a cautionary tale about the complexities such alliances can introduce.

Chapter 3: Charles and the Global Habsburg Empire

Maximilian became the Holy Roman emperor in 1493 and reigned until his death in 1519. His reign symbolizes a period of significant transition, marked by the waning influence of feudalism, the rise of centralized nation-states, and the burgeoning tension between emergent Renaissance humanism and enduring medieval chivalric ideals.

The Burgundian Inheritance

The original marriage contract between Maximilian and Mary gave the Habsburgs an enormous prize with consequences.

This inheritance was a double-edged sword. While it significantly expanded the Habsburgs' territorial and economic power, it also plunged Maximilian into the complex politics of the Low Countries and a protracted struggle with France, which contested the Burgundian legacy. Maximilian's reign was marked by near-constant military campaigns, most notably against the French and the Ottoman Empire. His struggles with France, ignited by the Burgundian inheritance, were characterized by shifting alliances and sporadic warfare, culminating in the Treaty of Senlis of 1493, which solidified Habsburg control over the Low Countries.

In the east, Maximilian faced the advancing Ottomans, who threatened Habsburg territories in Austria and Hungary. While not as directly involved as his successor would be, Maximilian's diplomatic and military efforts laid the groundwork for the Habsburg-Ottoman rivalry that would dominate European politics for centuries.

The Dawn of a New Era

Perhaps Maximilian's most enduring legacy is his administrative reforms and patronage of the arts and sciences, which deeply influenced the reign of his grandson, Charles V. Maximilian recognized the importance of a centralized administration to maintain his disparate territories. He reformed the existing institutions and laid the foundation for the Spanish Council of State and the Council of Finance in the Netherlands, which played crucial roles in Habsburg governance under Charles V.

Culturally, Maximilian was a key figure of the Northern Renaissance. His court was a haven for artists, musicians, and humanists. He commissioned works from Albrecht Dürer and Hans Burgkmair, among others, who created enduring visual representations of the emperor and his court. Maximilian's own writings, including his autobiographical *Der Weisskunig*, reflect both his chivalric ideals and his keen interest in the new humanist teachings.

Though Maximilian is often overshadowed by his grandson, Charles V, his legacy is evident in the realms of administrative reform, patronage of the arts, and the complex web of Habsburg territories that Charles would inherit.

Maximilian's era was one of both continuity and change, and his policies and actions left an indelible mark on the trajectory of European history. His efforts to maintain the autonomy of his territories while respecting local privileges and customs set a precedent for the delicate balance of centralized authority and regional autonomy that would characterize the reign of Charles V and the broader scope of European governance for centuries to come.

The Giant of the Era

In the annals of history, few figures loom as large as Holy Roman Emperor Charles V, ruler of the Spanish Empire and archduke of Austria. He was born in 1500 in Ghent, a thriving city within the Burgundian Netherlands. His life, fraught with incessant conflict, religious upheaval, and monumental responsibility, encapsulates the grandeur and complexity of the Habsburgs' global empire at its zenith.

Charles stood out in an age that produced Henry VIII of England, Francis I of France, and Suleman the Magnificent of the Ottoman Empire. The canvas of Charles's rule was vast and varied. He inherited an empire where, famously, the sun never set. His patrimony included the kingdoms of Castile, Aragon, and Navarre in Spain; the Burgundian territories in the Low Countries; vast Italian dominions, including Naples, Sicily, and Sardinia; and the burgeoning colonial realms in the Americas and the Philippines.

Yet, these were not peaceful realms dutifully passed from a dying father to a waiting son. Charles's inheritance was a patchwork of territories, each with its own distinct laws, traditions, and loyalties, stitched together by the dynastic marriages of his grandparents, Maximilian I and Mary of Burgundy and Ferdinand and Isabella, the famed Catholic Monarchs of Spain.

One of the greatest challenges Charles faced was the religious schism that threatened to tear Christendom asunder: the Protestant Reformation. Initiated by Martin Luther's *Ninety-five Theses* in 1517, the Reformation spread quickly due to the printing press and burgeoning nationalist sentiments. Charles's response was nuanced. While he summoned Luther to the Diet of Worms and later outlawed him, his focus on the larger political chessboard sometimes necessitated a more pragmatic approach. For instance, despite his Catholic fervor, he allied with Protestant princes against the Schmalkaldic League when political expediency demanded it.

Inheritance Acquisitions

Charles did not use the sword to acquire large tracts of land. He didn't have to; he inherited an enormous legacy. Charles was the son of Archduke Philip the Handsome, son of Holy Roman Emperor Maximilian I, and Joanna of Castile, daughter of Isabella I of Castile and Ferdinand II of Aragon. Charles gained the Habsburg Netherlands when his father died and was named co-ruler of Spain with his mother. When Joanna was declared mentally unfit to rule, Charles assumed the sole rule of Spain. By 1516, he was lord of the Netherlands and king of Spain and its New World possessions, as well as the monarch of Naples, Sicily, and Sardinia. He was only sixteen years old. When his paternal grandfather died, Charles was proclaimed the archduke of Austria.

A portrait of Charles V.

The Game of Imperial Succession

The death of Maximilian I in 1519 left the imperial throne of the Holy Roman Empire vacant. A new emperor had to be elected. Charles wanted to succeed his grandfather, but there were two others who also wanted to be the Holy Roman emperor: Francis I of France and Henry VIII of England. Henry's candidacy was not considered serious, but Francis was definitely interested in the imperial crown.

The French king was concerned about France being encircled by Habsburg possessions and wanted to disrupt any Habsburg schemes to dominate French borders. The French had an interest in Italy, and Francis briefly held Milan after his victory at Marignano in 1515. Francis wanted to extend French influence in the Italian Peninsula, particularly northern Italy. He could do that as Holy Roman emperor.

Charles had considerable resources at his disposal, thanks to his inheritances. However, getting the imperial crown was going to be a difficult challenge. The emperor was elected by the seven electors, but this was not democracy as we may think. It was an election based on bribery. The one who was able to make the right number of assurances and back those up with considerable sums of money was going to be the one to wear the crown.

France was a unified and wealthy country. King Francis I was going to be hard to beat, and Charles knew it. He had to summon extraordinary financial resources. So, he turned to an old ally.

A Modest Man of Incredible Wealth

A portrait of Jakob Fugger exists. It shows a man who dressed simply. There are no fabulous furs wrapped around his shoulders, nor are there eye-catching jewels on his fingers. Jakob Fugger did not have to impress anyone. Like Cosimo de Medici, who dressed modestly and did not try to draw attention, Fugger, who was the son of German merchants, had enormous amounts of money instead of fancy titles. He was a kingmaker who did not have to draw his sword.

Portrait of Jakob Fugger.
https://commons.wikimedia.org/wiki/File:Albrecht_D%C3%BCrer_080.jpg

Jakob Fugger was a businessman who knew the value of money and how to invest it. Fugger helped Archduke Sigmund of Austria pay his exorbitant debts when no other bankers would. Fugger was a reliable lender, but he was also a tough banker. The collateral for the debts was ownership of the Austrian silver mines, and Fugger was repaid for his loans with large amounts of silver. He eventually gained control of the state treasury.

Fugger became the banker of choice for the Habsburg family, and he loaned money to Maximilian I when the emperor needed it. Fugger would also become a significant lender to the popes.[8]

Fugger did a lot of business with the Habsburgs and wanted to continue his association with the dynasty. It would serve his own interests to have a client on the imperial throne.

Fugger's primary support was financial, as Charles did not have the liquid assets required to secure the votes of the electors. The German bankers supplied Charles with enormous sums of money to gain the support of the electors. The money would be used for financial incentives and gifts to the electors. The amount of money was staggering. Fugger's estimated financial support was approximately 850,000 florins.

This ally of Charles went even further. Jakob Fugger loaned money to very important people in Europe. His contacts and connections were considerable, so he could get the attention of the right people. Fugger pulled strings and used his contacts to gather support for Charles. He maneuvered vigorously, knowing that if Charles won, there would be huge prizes for him and his banking family.[9]

<u>The Concessions Charles Made</u>

Charles had to be willing to put up substantial collateral to gain the help of Jakob Fugger. These included the following:

- Territorial revenues: Charles was required to agree to offer revenues from lands within his possession as collateral.

---

[8] Getlen, L. (2015, July 26). Meet the World's Richest Man Who Changed Christianity. Retrieved from New York Post.com: https://nypost.com/2015/07/26/meet-historys-richest-man-who-changed-christianity/.

[9] Sorkin, A. D. (2015, September 11). How to Finance an Emperor's Election. Retrieved from The New Yorker: https://www.newyorker.com/news/amy-davidson/how-to-finance-an-emperors-election.

- Mining rights and monopolies: Charles granted Fugger mining rights within Habsburg possessions, particularly the copper and silver mines. The Fuggers would be allowed to operate mines and also have trade monopolies, such as the right to be the sole trader of certain commodities.
- Repayment with favorable terms: Charles was willing to repay the debts with more than just revenue from territories. The Fuggers would be allowed to collect taxes in certain cases and receive payments from imperial incomes. The interest rates on the loans were guaranteed.
- Protection: The Fuggers would become the primary creditor of the Holy Roman emperor. This also meant the Fuggers could rely on Charles for help if they ever got in trouble. These bankers could exert considerable influence because of their association with the emperor.[10]

The price for the support of the richest man in Europe was worth it. Charles won the election and became the Holy Roman emperor. He was the ruler of nearly all of central Europe. The title carried tremendous prestige but also great responsibilities. Charles was only nineteen when he was elected in 1519. He would be forced to deal with the greatest force of change Europe had experienced since the Roman Empire.

<u>The Monk Who Shook the World.</u>

Charles was elected Holy Roman emperor on June 28th, 1519; he would be formally crowned by Pope Clement V on February 24th, 1530. He emerged from the election as the most powerful man in Europe, master of the largest European empire of the last one thousand years.

Charles had little time to celebrate this success. An event that happened on October 15th, 1517, would cast a long shadow on his reign.

There was nothing remarkable about Martin Luther. He was an Augustinian monk and a theologian who taught at the University of Wittenberg. He was a man of deep thoughts and concern about his salvation. Luther was also very alert to the corruption and abuses of the Roman Catholic Church. He was horrified by the sale of plenary indulgences that Johann Tetzel was using to raise money for the construction of the new St. Peter's Basilica. Tetzel's marketing slogan,

---

[10] Heath, R. (2023, October 21). Emperor Charles V and the Fugger Family. Retrieved from Emperor Charles V: https://www.emperorcharlesv.com/charles-v-fugger-family/.

"As soon as the coin in the coffer rings, the soul from purgatory springs," was very offensive to Luther.

Martin Luther was brave enough to speak out. He opposed the sale of indulgences and other contemporary church practices. To him, only God could forgive sins; indulgences had no effect on a person's salvation. While it is not certain whether Luther physically nailed the *Ninety-five Theses* expressing his views on the door of All Saints' Church in Wittenberg, he did write to the local bishop in October 1517. He included his work, *Disputation of the Power and Efficacy of Indulgences*, which were to become known as the *Ninety-five Theses*.

Portrait of Martin Luther.

A normal reaction of the authorities to Martin Luther would be to shrug their shoulders. After all, the church had dealt with self-proclaimed reformers before. If things got out of hand, these people would be excommunicated and, like Jan Hus, executed and their followers persecuted.

Martin Luther was different. Unlike earlier dissidents, Luther had a powerful weapon at his disposal, which he was going to use. It was the printing press.

The Power of the Printed Word

The invention of Johannes Gutenberg, the printing press, transformed Europe. The printing press could produce printed works faster than ever before. Thus, Luther could spread multiple copies of his work without having to wait months for someone to painstakingly do it by hand. Martin Luther and other Protestant reformers exploited the capabilities of the printing press to get their arguments and new religious beliefs to thousands.

Messages like Martin Luther's insistence on salvation by faith alone or John Calvin's predestination could be spread easily and in multiple places, allowing these men to gain thousands of followers among the common people and the nobility alike. The printing press allowed the reformers to communicate directly with the populace, bypassing the traditional authority structures of the Catholic Church and the Holy Roman Empire. This direct line to the masses provided a platform for dissent and allowed for the questioning of long-established doctrines and practices. The old order was in serious trouble.

A Serious Challenge to the Status Quo

The Roman Catholic Church's power was heavily predicated on its control over religious knowledge and interpretation. The printing press enabled the laity to access religious texts, including vernacular Bibles, thereby undermining the church's monopoly on religious matters. The spread of Protestant ideas contributed to the fragmentation of Christendom. This was a direct threat to the Catholic Church's claim of being the universal church, diminishing its spiritual authority and temporal power.

Charles V ruled over lands that were held together tenuously by custom and the Catholic Church. Protestant dissent threatened the political stability of the empire and challenged his ability to govern a diverse and increasingly divided populace. The printing press was used not only for religious texts but also for pamphlets and broadsheets that criticized imperial governance. A surge in anti-clerical and anti-imperial sentiment, readily visible in printed materials, stoked public dissent.

Charles tried to find some amicable way to bring both sides of the religious contest together. He allowed Martin Luther the opportunity in

1521 to defend his ideas at the Diet of Worms. Luther did not recant his writings, so Charles had to do something. What he did was issue the Edict of Worms, which rejected Luther's doctrines and placed the Habsburgs firmly against the forces of Protestantism.[11]

Charles made another effort to try to reach conciliation. He summoned German princes in 1530 to the Diet of Augsburg to end the religious struggles. Instead, something more radical, the Confession of Augsburg, was submitted to Charles. The Confession of Augsburg was a profession of the Protestant faith that clarified the Protestants' position on various religious topics. The document was rejected by Charles. On November 19th, 1530, the Diet issued a verdict that gave Protestant princes six months to renounce their new religion. That did not happen.[12]

Charles viewed the Protestant Reformation as a threat and worked tirelessly to bring it to an end. He tried political maneuvering, and then he decided to use military campaigns to force upstart Protestant princes back into the church. His most significant enemy was the Schmalkaldic League, an alliance of Protestant princes. The league was dedicated to defending the Reformation. Charles defeated the league at the Battle of Mühlberg in 1547, but it was an expensive victory. Charles was facing major threats from the Ottoman Empire and France. He could not fight religious wars and secular disputes at the same time. Ultimately, he had to compromise.

The Peace of Augsburg of 1555 allowed the coexistence of Catholicism and Lutheranism in the Holy Roman Empire. It created an interesting legal term, "cuius regio, eius religio" ("whose land, his religion"). It means that the religion of the local ruler would dictate the religion of those whom he ruled.

The Peace of Augsburg provided an end to the religious conflict and also acknowledged the permanent religious division in Europe. The days of the Roman Catholic Church as the sole arbiter of theological matters were over. It was hard for Charles to accept this, but he had other matters to face that were more troublesome. His borders were not very secure.

---

[11] Ferdinand, M. d. (2023, September 17). Charles V Holy Roman Emperor. Retrieved from Britannica.com: https://www.britannica.com/biography/Charles-V-Holy-Roman-emperor.

[12] Musee Protestant. (2023, October 21). The Augsburg Confession (1530). Retrieved from Museeprotestant.org: https://museeprotestant.org/en/notice/the-augsburg-confession-1530/.

The French and Ottoman Threats

Francis I was an implacable enemy of Charles. The French king was constantly probing for a way to checkmate the Habsburgs and increase the influence of France. The Habsburg-Valois Wars against France were particularly draining, both financially and personally. These conflicts, which spanned Charles's entire reign, were a chess game for control of Italy and preeminence in Europe.

Italy was a testing ground for the two nations. France made incursions into Italy with the hopes of challenging the hegemony of the Habsburgs. The Battle of Pavia in 1525 was a decisive victory for Charles. The French were defeated, and Francis was captured. He became a prisoner and signed the Treaty of Madrid in 1526, in which he renounced all his claims in Italy.

The threat of the Ottoman Empire was another constant preoccupation. The advances of Suleiman the Magnificent in central Europe culminated in the siege of Vienna in 1529. Though the siege was unsuccessful, it marked the beginning of a protracted struggle between the Habsburgs and the Ottomans. Charles's response was a mix of military opposition and pragmatic diplomacy, as seen in his correspondence, where he weighed the costs of war against the benefits of temporary peace.

The Twilight

Exhausted by decades of warfare and diplomacy and suffering from severe gout, Charles abdicated in a series of steps from 1554 to 1556, dividing his empire between his son, Philip II, King of Spain, and his brother, Ferdinand I, Holy Roman Emperor. His abdication letters evoke a man weary of the burden of power and who sought solace in faith. He retired to the Monastery of Yuste in Spain, where he died in 1558.

The Final Word on a Significant Reign

Charles ruled over a far-flung empire. It could months to go from one place to another. The Habsburgs had possessions on five continents: Europe, Africa, Asia, South America, and North America.

To administer these vast dominions, Charles employed a mix of traditional Habsburg dynastic strategies and innovative bureaucratic mechanisms. He frequently traveled, understanding the importance of presence as a means of asserting authority. His itinerary, as recorded in letters and court documents, was grueling, yet it reflects his commitment to direct oversight. His personal correspondence reveals a keen intellect and a detail-oriented ruler. He often delved into minutiae that would seem below the notice of an emperor.

Those letters also show how Charles marveled at the quantities of gold and silver in the Americas, as these precious metals offered him the financial means to maintain his far-flung territories and fund his numerous military campaigns. Managing distant colonies required a delicate balancing act. In his correspondence with colonial administrators, Charles emphasized the conversion of indigenous peoples to Christianity, though these missives also betray a ruthless pragmatism, as he condoned harsh measures to ensure the colonies' profitability.

Charles V's Legacy

Charles V's reign represents the Habsburg dynasty's high watermark. Under his stewardship, the disparate lands under Habsburg rule were, for the first time, united under a single ruler. However, his reign also sowed the seeds of future challenges. The financial strains of constant warfare and the difficulties in governing diverse territories foreshadowed troubles that would plague his successors.

His legacy is complex. To his detractors, he was an autocrat whose staunch defense of Catholicism led to decades of religious warfare. To his supporters, he was a visionary ruler who sought to maintain Christian unity and imperial stability amid unprecedented challenges.

Whatever view you take, Charles V was a colossus, straddling the worlds of the Middle Ages and the Renaissance, of feudal lordships and nation-states, of regional kingships and global empires. His reign, marked by both triumph and tragedy, encapsulates the grandeur, complexity, and, ultimately, the fragility of the Habsburg global empire.

Chapter 4: The Wealth of the New World

The sun never set on the lands held by the Habsburgs. That is not poetic license but an actual fact. It took centuries for the Habsburgs to acquire the territories they owned in 1510. It took less than a century to assume sovereignty over possessions that spanned the globe. It was an international empire and the first of its kind.

Traditional empires covered landmasses. For example, the Roman Empire controlled land in Europe, Asia, and Africa, but land connections enabled relatively easy access to all the provinces. What the Habsburgs held by the end of the 16th century was thousands of miles apart. Manila was more than ten thousand miles away from Madrid. Traveling from Mexico City to Lima, Peru, would take months. However, the colonial empire included staggering wealth to be exploited.

<u>Conquistadors</u>

Much of the Habsburg Empire was in the New World. The expansion began when Christopher Columbus landed in the Bahamas. Hernán Cortés then landed in Mexico and defeated the Aztecs by the time Charles V was crowned Holy Roman emperor (remember, he was also the king of Spain and the ruler of various other territories). This remarkable accomplishment was performed by a special breed of men known as conquistadors.

These soldiers of fortune were drawn primarily from the Iberian Peninsula and were adventurers looking for considerable wealth and everlasting fame. They were military types who had seen action in the European wars. It is wrong to think they were illiterate because many had classical educations in Latin and Greek, as well as specialized studies in mathematics. They came from all classes of society. The conquistadors were not knights in shining armor nor valiant warriors made famous by the songs of troubadours. Instead, these men were, by and large, violent and ruthless individuals who did not hesitate to use extreme means to get what they wanted. Greed was one of their greatest motivators.

Cortés and Pizarro

The two best-known conquistadors were Hernán Cortés and Francisco Pizarro. Both men were able to conquer significant empires in the New World with relatively few men. People are amazed at how these two men were able to do so much when the odds were definitely not in their favor. The best explanation is that Cortés and Pizarro were in the right place at the right time.

For instance, there is the claim that the Aztecs thought Cortés was the god Quetzalcoatl, whose return had been the stuff of legends in central Mexico. Pizzaro arrived in Peru after the Inca Empire had been exhausted by internal disputes and civil war. The two men took advantage of the military technology they had, which the natives did not, but that was not the only method they employed.

The Aztecs and the Incas had been tyrants who could be incredibly cruel to their subjects. Cortés was aided in his final assault of the Aztec capital, Tenochtitlan, by thousands of indigenous allies who saw an opportunity to destroy their Aztec overlords. Pizarro made strategic alliances with South American tribes, including the Huancas, Chankas, Cañaris, and Chacahpoyas. These tribes furnished troops for the conquistadors. When these indigenous tribes realized they had supplanted one tyrant for another, it was too late.

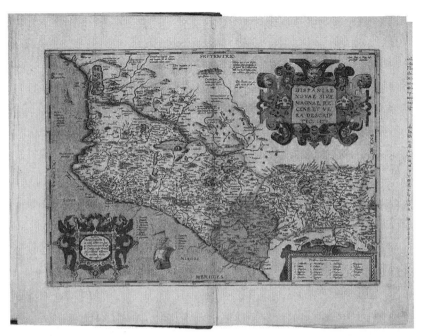

A map of New Spain made in the early 1600s.
https://commons.wikimedia.org/wiki/File:Map_of_New_Spain_by_Abraham_Ortelius.jpeg

While Hernán Cortés and Francisco Pizarro are among the most well-known conquistadors, there were others who made significant contributions to Spanish colonization efforts. In addition to being conquerors, these men were explorers who discovered lands and cultures unknown to Europeans. Here are some of the most famous conquistadors and the lands they conquered:

• Hernando de Soto

Hernando de Soto led an expedition through what is now the southeastern United States between 1539 and 1542. His journey took him through regions such as Florida, Georgia, Alabama, and Mississippi, adding to Europe's knowledge of North America. His expedition was significant in opening up the interior of the continent.

• Pedro de Alvarado

Pedro de Alvarado was a key lieutenant of Cortés during the conquest of Mexico. He would lead his own expedition into Central America, where he played a primary role in the conquest of what is now Guatemala, Honduras, and El Salvador.

• Vasco Núñez de Balboa

Vasco Núñez de Balboa is best known for being the first European to cross the Isthmus of Panama. He discovered the Pacific Ocean in 1513.

• Álvar Núñez Cabeza de Vaca

Cabeza de Vaca was a member of an ill-fated expedition to Florida led by Pánfilo de Narváez. After surviving shipwrecks and hardship, he embarked on an epic journey across the Gulf Coast and into the American Southwest. He was one of the first Europeans to explore those regions.

These conquistadors and others played vital roles in expanding the Spanish Empire across a vast portion of the Americas, leaving a lasting legacy that included cultural exchange, colonization, and the exchange of goods and ideas between the Old World and the New World.

<u>In the Sign of the Cross</u>

Charles V insisted that any conquered people in the New World were to be brought to Christ and baptized as Christians. Dominicans and Franciscans went to the Americas just for this purpose. Their objective was to evangelize the new subjects. That appears to be a noble idea, but conversion was unfortunately mingled with suppression. Many indigenous people were forced into Christianity.

The subjugation in the name of Christ was not ignored even back then. Priests and monks noticed the savagery of the conquistadors and the avarice of those who governed the native population. The chief critic was Bartolomé de las Casas. He reported back to Spain about the treatment of these new subjects. Those letters, combined with those of other observers, were shocking. Charles V was among those who were disgusted by what they read.

An outcome of the outrage was the Valladolid debate. These took place in Valladolid, Spain, on August 15th, 1550, and centered on the abuse of the indigenous people who lived in New Spain. The result of the debate was a decision that the natives deserved the same rights and privileges enjoyed by Europeans. De las Casas published a book, *A Short Account of the Destruction of the Indies*, that shed light on the terrible treatment of the native peoples. The conquistadors could not hide behind the cross anymore.[13]

---

[13] History Skills. (2023, September 14). The Valladolid Debate: When Europeans Argued About

Philip II, who succeeded Charles, would define future Spanish discoveries as pacifications, not conquests. Still, considerable damage had been done, and many indigenous people suffered. Their treatment remains a sad legacy to this day.

Governing the New World

Governing the immense possessions of the New World with its numerous nationalities was a challenge. The Council of the Indies was created in 1524 to oversee the new colonies. The Spanish Habsburgs divided up the territory of New Spain into viceroyalties. Viceroys governed these administrative units. They represented the Spanish Crown and were answerable to the Spanish king. However, given the distance between the Americas and Madrid, the viceroys had considerable autonomy in daily affairs. Maintaining order in the colony was their primary responsibility.

Beneath them was an administrative system that was intended to guarantee that the colonies were productive. The encomienda system was initially used to keep the land and its inhabitants productive for the sake of the Crown. It was a method of land distribution where Spanish settlers, encomenderos, were given land grants. They gave the settlers control over the local indigenous people. The encomenderos were given the responsibility of providing religious instruction, protection, and fair treatment to the native people, who were expected to provide free labor as tribute. As you may have already guessed, what usually happened was that the indigenous people were exploited.

De las Casas and his associates showcased the abuses of this system. The Spanish government tried to reform it. The repartimiento system was created to take the place of the encomienda system. This system was intended to regulate the use of the native population so they could be treated more fairly. It required an indigenous person to work a set number of days per year on assignments such as mining. The repartimiento system did provide a certain amount of protection.

The Roman Catholic Church played a significant role in the Americas. Its basic mission was to convert the native population to Christianity. Missions were established throughout the Spanish New World. They were both religious centers and agricultural hubs. The

---

Whether Indigenous People Were Human. Retrieved from Historyskills.com:
https://www.historyskills.com/classroom/year-8/valladolid-debate/.

treatment of native peoples was more humane under the guidance of the church. Other efforts to moderate the treatment of the native populations included the Laws of the Indies and the New Laws.

This did not mean that the indigenous populations were free from all abuse or exploitation. The Americas were a rich territory, and the Spanish were intent on exploiting all of it. The populations of the indigenous people suffered as a result. Many succumbed to either European diseases or the backbreaking labor they were forced to provide for the sake of their overlords.

An enduring legacy of the Spanish Habsburgs in the New World was the gift of language. Spanish was the lingua franca of New Spain, and it supplanted the various languages spoken in the Americas. It was not long before a person could travel from the Rio Grande to Tierra del Fuego, a distance of over six thousand miles, and be understood most of the way. Spanish was a valuable commercial tool.

The Trade Routes

The wealth the Spanish extracted from the New World was staggering. The amount of mined gold and silver bullion had no comparable figures in European history. It is hard to pinpoint precisely how much was taken from the ground during the days of the Spanish Empire. It is known from the registered trade accounts that between 1500 and 1650, 181 tons of gold and 16,000 tons of silver went from the Americas to Spain. The need to safely export these precious commodities to Europe created various trade routes.[14]

The Voyage of the Flotas

Single vessels were prey to pirates, so a system was developed that would permit convoys to cross the Atlantic. These were the Spanish treasure fleets known as flotas. The best-known flota was the Flota de Indias, supervised by the Casa de Contratación (House of Trade of the Indies), which would sail from Veracruz in Mexico to Seville. Many ships arrived safely, but there were instances where the flotas were caught in hurricanes and sunk. Archaeologists and treasure hunters have been dredging up cargoes from these lost ships, and the value of what was carried in them is in the millions of dollars. The findings represent only

---

[14] Encyclopedia.com. (2023, October 25). Mining, The Americas. Retrieved from Encyclopedia.com: https://www.encyclopedia.com/history/encyclopedias-almanacs-transcripts-and-maps/mining-americas.

a fraction of what was in the holds of treasure ships that left port and headed to Spain.

The Camino Real and the Inca Roads

Most mines were located in remote areas, such as the mountains of northern Mexico. Gold bullion had to be transported to the coast, so the Spanish created a network of commercial roads. The Camino Real was one that connected mines in Zacatecas to Mexico City. From there, the gold would be sent to Veracruz.

The Spanish also made use of the existing Inca road system in South America. These paths were expanded to allow the transportation of resources. The roads not only permitted treasure to be sent to Europe. They also helped economic development in Spanish America, with goods going back and forth along the trails.

There is a story about the movement of precious metals in the New World that is not very well known but is fascinating nonetheless. It is not a legend but a fact that the silver extracted by the Spanish was in extraordinary quantities. Modern visitors to Mexico and South America can see for themselves that the amount of silver was so enormous that it was used for ordinary decorations in numerous churches and holy places. The intriguing story of silver from the New World is that the metal did not always flow east to Europe. Large quantities also sailed west.

The Spanish discovered deposits of silver in Mexico, but the motherlode was not in North America; it was in South America. In 1545, an indigenous person named Diego Gualpa discovered a vein of silver in the Bolivian Andes. It was the purest quality of silver ever seen. Gualpa made his discovery in a mountain that was over fifteen thousand feet high. Further explorations confirmed that what Gualpa uncovered was the stuff of legends and fairy tales. It was more than just one trace of silver: the Andean native had discovered a mountain of silver.

It is the stuff of fairy tales, but the silver mountain was real. The Spanish named it Cerro Rico ("Rich Mountain"), and Potosí was the name of the mining town established to dig the silver out of the mountainside. The find was beyond words to describe accurately. Charles V came close by calling Potosí the "treasury of the world." Between 1545 and 1810, Potosí produced almost 20 percent of the silver in the world. Its production effectively ended any lack of silver in

Europe.[15]

So, why did any of it go west instead of east? An imperial decree caused that to happen.

China had relied for centuries on an in-kind form of taxation (taxes paid with goods or services rather than money), and the government relied on grain and labor to secure needed revenue. It was inefficient, and changes needed to be made. In 1581, the Ming dynasty decreed that all taxes would be paid in silver. That was a more effective way of getting the money for needed public projects. However, the difficulty was that China itself did not have large deposits of silver. It had to be imported from someplace else.

Potosí was the solution to that problem. South American silver could be exported to China, and a westward trade route was born out of the Chinese demand for silver bullion.

A fleet of silver-bearing ships left Acapulco, Mexico, twice a year to sail across the Pacific Ocean until it reached Manila in the Spanish-held Philippines. Manila became the contact point for exchanging silver for Chinese products, such as silk and ceramics. The trade route operated from 1565 to 1815, gathering momentum as the years passed.[16]

China received silver imports from Japan, but these fell off in the 17th century. Potosí became the primary source of what the Ming dynasty needed. Manila became the permanent trade link between the Americas and Asia.

The Habsburgs extracted ore from their colonies in the New World, and the wealth they achieved was staggering. However, there was a dark side to the picture. The Habsburgs faced problems in Europe and were required to be proactive in defending their territory and ambitions. Some of the issues might have been quickly resolved if diplomacy were used.

However, the Habsburg New World riches made the dynasty overconfident. They believed they could settle their problems with

---

[15] Maxwell, K. (2020, December 30). The Beginnings of Globalization: The Spanish Silver Trade Routes. Retrieved from Defense.info: https://defense.info/global-dynamics/2020/12/the-beginnings-of-globalization-the-spanish-silver-trade-routes/.

[16] Sun, L. (2020, Fall). Late Imperial China, Silver, and Global Trade Routes. Retrieved from Association for Asian Studies: https://www.asianstudies.org/publications/eaa/archives/late-imperial-china-silver-and-global-trade-routes/.

military force. They had the money to afford large armadas and armies and felt they could overcome obstacles with pure force. It was a terrible mistake. The Habsburgs would discover that all the silver mined in South America could not sufficiently cover the expense of conducting military campaigns that produced few positive results and assured only destruction and death.

Chapter 5: The Ottoman-Habsburg War

Charles V divided his empire in 1556 when he abdicated. Spain and the western Habsburg territories went to his son Philip. His brother Ferdinand received Austria and the Holy Roman Empire. Ferdinand had already been elected king of the Romans in 1531 and was formally recognized as the Holy Roman emperor in 1558. He had ruled the Austrian lands of the Habsburgs in his brother's name and had the additional titles of archduke of Austria and king of Hungary, Croatia, and Bohemia.

Charles's decision was a pragmatic one based on his own experiences. He felt it was not possible for one man to rule over all the Habsburg possessions. This division permitted his two successors to focus their attention on their areas while keeping everything within the dynasty. It was a smart move. Ferdinand was able to provide close attention to a formidable enemy who was threatening Europe from the southeast.

The Ottomans were a force to be reckoned with. They steadily chipped away at what was left of the Byzantine Empire until, in 1453, they seized Constantinople. Their aggression did not stop there. The Ottomans gradually worked their way through the Balkans and, on August 29th, 1526, decisively defeated the Hungarians at the Battle of Mohács. These Muslim imperialists were now on the border of Habsburg land.

The Magnificent One

The Habsburgs faced the most extraordinary sultan of the Ottoman Empire: Suleiman the Magnificent. Suleiman ruled the Ottoman Empire when it was at its zenith, and he stretched the borders to its furthest point. He was devoted to spreading Islam through conquest, and he intended to confront and eventually defeat his Christian rivals. Suleman's victory at Mohács gave him control over Hungary and Transylvania. He then decided to campaign against Archduke Ferdinand.

Suleiman marched an army of more than 100,000 men into Austria in May 1529. He was at a disadvantage because of the rainy weather, and the mud forced him to leave behind heavy artillery pieces. The Ottoman army was able to reach Vienna by September, but the weather still caused problems. The heavy rains dampened the Ottomans' gunpowder. Suleiman was forced to retreat and lost thousands of men by withdrawing in the winter. A second attempt to seize Vienna failed in 1532.[17]

The reversals in Vienna were the first time European opposition had effectively stymied the Ottomans. It proved there were logistical challenges that the Ottomans had to confront when invading deep into Europe; extending supply lines beyond the Ottoman core territories was a problem for the empire.

Wars on the eastern front with Persia forced Suleiman to draw his attention away from Europe, but it did not mean he had lost interest. The Ottomans and the Habsburgs would fight another day.

Charles V tested the Ottoman Empire's might in North Africa and came away disappointed. He intended to fulfill the dream of his grandfather, Ferdinand of Aragon, to conquer North Africa and defeat the Ottoman corsair Barbarossa. Charles captured Tunis in 1535 and commanded an expedition against Algiers in 1541. It was a disaster, and over twelve thousand Habsburg soldiers and sailors were killed. Charles's ventures in North Africa did not accomplish any lasting results, and Ottoman pirates were able to continue raiding European coasts and disrupting maritime commerce.

The Siege of Malta

The Ottomans wanted control of the western Mediterranean, and the island of Malta stood in their way. Sulieman had a personal interest in

---

[17] Parry, V. (2023, October 25). Suleyman the Magnificent. Retrieved from Britannica.com: https://www.britannica.com/biography/Suleyman-the-Magnificent.

taking Malta that went beyond imperial designs. The military order that controlled Malta was originally the Knights Hospitaller. The sultan had defeated this Christian order in the siege of Rhodes in 1523 and permitted the surviving Christian knights to leave without harm. Charles gave Malta and the neighboring islands to the order, and they changed their name to the Knights of Malta. They then began harassing Ottoman shipping. Suleman was determined to settle old scores at long last. He sailed with a force of 40,000 men and a fleet of 250 ships to take Malta.

Malta was more than an island; it was a floating fortress. The harbor was fortified, and the city of Valletta had high walls and substantial fortifications. It was a tremendous challenge, and the Knights of Malta were determined to resist the Ottoman invaders. The attack would prove costly.

The siege began on May 18th, 1565. The knights were outnumbered by more than five to one, but they held on for four months until a Spanish relief force landed on September 7th, 1565, and forced the Ottomans to abandon the siege. Objectively, the siege of Malta was a waste of time for Suleiman and his Ottoman troops. The sultan could have considered far more critical areas for assault and conquest, such as Sardinia. Precious time and troops had been wasted.

The siege of Malta.
https://commons.wikimedia.org/wiki/File:Matteo_Perez_d%27_Aleccio_(1547-1616)_-_The_Siege_of_Malta,_Attack_on_the_Post_of_the_Castilian_Knights,_21_August_1565_-_BHC0257_-_Royal_Museums_Greenwich.jpg

New Rulers, New Approaches

Charles V was dead and gone by the time of the siege of Malta. Suleiman himself lived only for a few more years after the siege. The son of Charles, Philip II, was now leading the Spanish Habsburgs. Holy Roman Emperor Ferdinand I had died in 1564. His successor, Maximilian II, was crowned Holy Roman emperor that year. Maximilian was more tolerant than other Habsburgs. He permitted some degree of tolerance to Lutherans without granting all their demands, which was still a welcome change from earlier years.

Maximilian did not hesitate to protect his borders from Ottoman incursions, but he was also open to negotiation. He concluded the Austrian-Turkish War (1566–1568) by negotiating a peace treaty with Suleiman's successor, Selim II. The Treaty of Adrianople was signed on February 17th, 1568. Maximilian agreed to give the sultan an annual gift of thirty thousand ducats and recognized Ottoman authority in Transylvania, Moldavia, and Wallachia. What Maximilian received in return was relative peace for the next twenty-five years. This allowed both sides to concentrate on other matters, including internal difficulties. The peace may have been one of the reasons why Maximilian was not involved in the greatest naval battle of the 16th century.

The Battle of Lepanto

The Battle of Lepanto was the most significant naval engagement of its time. It pitted Christian Europe against the Ottoman Empire at a time when the Ottomans were at the height of their power. It was also the last battle where the galleys played a significant role.

The Christian Holy League was led by Spain under Philip II. Philips's nephew, Don Juan of Austria, commanded the Christian fleet. The Christians and the Ottomans met in combat on October 7th, 1571. The Christians used superior military technology and tactics to defeat the larger Ottoman fleet.

Although the victory did not mean that the Ottomans were no longer a power to be reckoned with in military affairs, the win was a significant morale boost for western Europe. It marked the beginning of the slow decline of the Ottoman Empire. The legacy of Lepanto can be found in the art, poetry, and theater of the 16th century. It was seen as a decisive Habsburg victory.

The contest between the Habsburgs and the Ottomans showcased the military technology and diplomacy of the 16th century. It was a classic struggle between two opposing religions and ideologies, and the consequences shaped the history of central and eastern Europe for the next three centuries and into the modern era. We can better understand the struggle by examining the military innovations, treaties, and political changes that resulted from these two opposing forces colliding.

It was a see-saw relationship. One side would have the upper hand for some time, and then the other side would come out on top. It created a unique situation where, at one point, Christian France entered into an alliance with Ottoman Turkey to check the aspirations of the Habsburgs.

Peace treaties were often signed to give both sides some breathing room and the opportunity to address other more pressing issues within their borders. Such interludes were temporary. A few years might pass, and then the armies were on the march against each other. Lands would change hands as the strategic chess game went back and forth.

Siege warfare was prominent in the wars of the 16th century. Major cities and locations would be heavily defended and attacked by superior forces. Starving out the garrison or using diplomacy combined with treachery were often the means of ending these encounters, which would usually last for months or even years. The Ottomans developed a siege war strategy that enabled them to overcome defenses and end a siege within a reasonable period of time.

The siege of Constantinople in 1453 introduced western Europe to Ottoman siege tactics. Constantinople's walls permitted it to resist repeated attempts to take the city. These were massive bastions with walls that were several feet thick and towered above opposing forces.

The Ottomans used siege artillery to batter the walls of the Byzantine capital. These war machines eventually helped create a breach in the wall that led to the capture of the city. The Ottomans would continue to use specialized artillery in siege warfare.

The siege cannons were known as the Ottoman bombards. These monsters could be anywhere from six to seventeen tons in weight and hurl cannonballs weighing as much as seven hundred pounds. The Ottomans became highly proficient in gunpowder strategy, and the Balkans were their testing grounds.

Bombards were larger than contemporary artillery and were often cased on-site. Cannon foundries were established throughout the Balkans to furnish the needed ordnance. The Ottomans originally cast them from iron and then later used a single-piece bronze construction, which permitted greater durability and firepower. The bombard was used in addition to traditional sapping activities to undermine solid walls.[18]

The Ottomans also used psychological warfare to undermine the morale of the defenders. Drumming was a viable tool, and the deafening noise from other instruments created auditory confusion. The Ottomans were not averse to displaying the severed heads of enemies within sight of a besieged city's walls. We may think that is dreadful, but Christian armies used the same tactic.

Habsburg Defenses

The Habsburgs were hammered by the Ottomans in the early 16th century but learned how to respond more effectively to their Muslim adversary. A border defense system was created that had a string of fortresses built along the border from the Adriatic Sea to Transylvania. There were significant forts whose garrisons were as large as 1,500 troops, castles with garrisons of 400 to 600 men, and smaller stone and hard-fence castles with 100 to 300 soldiers. These could slow down most Ottoman advances and give the Habsburgs time to raise additional forces.[19]

The Habsburgs also used a series of sophisticated fortifications to frustrate the attempts of their enemies. Their defensive walls were ordinarily thick stone masonry that could withstand ordinary artillery fire. The fortifications were not always basic curtain walls, though. Bastions were angular protrusions in the wall that could cover more ground with rifle fire and offered better angles of defense.

Ravelins came into use as the years progressed. These were triangular fortifications positioned in front of the main walls and were additional barriers that often included cannons. Redoubts were small, heavily fortified strong points within much more extensive fortifications and were placed to provide heightened defense at critical junctures.

---

[18] Mediakron.bc.edu. (2023, October 25). Turkish Bombard. Retrieved from Mediakron.bc.edu: https://mediakron.bc.edu/ottomans/turkish-bombard/siege-of-vienna.

[19] Palffy, G. (2002). The Border Defense System in Hungary in the Sixteenth and Seventeenth Centuries. Retrieved from Academia.edu: https://www.academia.edu/539595/The_Border_Defense_System_in_Hungary_in_the_Sixteenth_and_Seventeenth_Centuries_In_A_Millennium_of_Hungarian_Military_History_Ed_L%C3%A1szl%C3%B3_Veszpr%C3%A9my_B%C3%A9la_K_Kir%C3%A1ly_New_York_Social_Science_Monographs_Bro.

Habsburg defenses also included artillery platforms.

Naval Technology

The Battle of Lepanto showcased advances in technology and strategy that worked to the advantage of the Habsburgs. The galleass was the battle wagon that broke the back of the Ottoman fleet. These were massive ships whose crews numbered in the hundreds. They were armed with as many as fifty artillery pieces, with heavy guns mounted in the stern and in the bow of the vessel. The galleass was a floating artillery battery that presaged the enormous man-of-war ships that were common in the 18th century.[20]

Infantry Comparisons

The Ottomans and the Habsburgs relied on professional armies whose soldiers were not farmers called up for thirty days of service. Instead, the Ottomans used the Janissaries as their shock troops, and the Habsburg relied on the Landsknechts. Both the Janissaries and the Landsknechts were professional soldiers.

Ottoman tactics relied on the use of firepower, and the Habsburgs used tight formations that were defensive as opposed to offensive. Both sides relied on sophisticated battlefield tactics. The days of the mass rush were coming to a close. These two rivals made use of the best technology and superior weapons, and both could overwhelm poorly organized enemies.

Diplomacy

Treaties were signed between the Ottomans and the Habsburgs. We can think of these as intermezzos that separated major periods of conflict. The treaties allowed both sides to recover from intense combat and repair damage. However, peace between the two sides was a fleeting moment in time. From the 16th to the 19th centuries, the Habsburgs and the Ottomans battled it out for supremacy in central and southeastern Europe. Some of the diplomatic pacts were more significant than others.

The Treaty of Constantinople, signed in 1533, marked the end of the initial phase of hostilities between the Habsburgs and the Ottomans. What is interesting about this document is the subtle slaps administered by the Ottomans to their enemy. Archduke Ferdinand of Austria was required to recognize Sulieman as his suzerain and needed to pay tribute

---

[20] Serlin, D. (2014, May 1). Turning the Tide: Venetian Contributions to the Battle of Lepanto. Retrieved from Vtuhr.org: https://vtuhr.org/articles/10.21061/vtuhr.v3i0.21.

to the sultan every year. Ferdinand was compelled to renounce claims to all of Hungary except for a western portion. The treaty referred to Charles V as the king of Spain, and Charles was not permitted to call anyone, including himself, "emperor" except Sulieman. For all the pomp and circumstances surrounding the treaty, Sulieman declared the treaty invalid a few years later, and the peace officially ended in 1537 with the Battle of Gorjani.

Modern readers must remember that these treaties are not comparable to the Treaty of Versailles. They were not really documents between a victor and the vanquished. The Habsburgs were making concessions that were considered necessary at that moment. The family was still in control of the Holy Roman Empire, and the monarch of the Spanish Empire was still a Habsburg. What was lost in one treaty could be quickly regained several years later as a result of a successful military campaign.

The Spanish and the Austrian Habsburgs were in almost constant war during the 16th century. The Ottomans happened to be their primary rival, but there were internal revolts and disputes with the Protestants that kept these monarchs incredibly busy. It is to the credit of the Habsburgs that they could withstand enormous pressure and remain the principal ruling family in Europe.

The conflict would not end until the 18th century. Both sides suffered decline due to the lengthy war, which allowed other powers like Britain and France to gain power and challenge the Habsburgs on the world stage. However, the war did end somewhat favorably for the Habsburgs, as they were able to add Hungary and Transylvania to their empire.

Chapter 6: Arts, Sciences, and Habsburg Patronage

The Habsburgs dominated central Europe culturally and politically. The Habsburgs were more than aristocrats who built monasteries so that monks could pray for their blue-blooded souls. Habsburg princes, kings, and emperors were full-blooded patrons of the arts. Their support shaped two significant cultural movements: the Renaissance and the Baroque period.

The Council of Trent played a dominant role in developing the arts. This council created guidelines that told the artists how they could paint religious art. The Council of Trent provided instructions for other areas as well, such as architecture. The Habsburgs were devout Catholics and paid attention to the new guidelines.

There are some differences between what the Spanish and the Austrian Habsburgs did to affect culture. We are going to look at each one and explain how each branch of the family influenced the arts.

Spanish Habsburgs

Art

The Spanish Habsburgs significantly influenced the culture of the Late Renaissance and Baroque period. Their governance was a combination of political power, religious zeal, and artistic patronage. They were staunch defenders of Catholicism, and Charles V's successor, Philip II, followed a rigorous policy of promoting the Catholic faith and fighting what he considered to be Protestant heresy.

A commitment to realism and naturalism characterized Spanish painting under the Habsburgs. The artists employed by the Habsburgs worked to depict the world with accuracy, detail, and precision. Portraiture became a prominent genre, and the Spanish Habsburgs used paintings to project their power and prestige.

Mysticism is evident in the Spanish works of this time. El Greco's art was influenced by his Greek heritage. A viewer can see elements of Byzantine art and a sense of spiritual transcendence in his work.

- El Greco

El Greco was the most prominent Spanish painter. His work showed a dramatic and expressive style that many people at the time could not understand. El Greco studied under Titian and moved to Spain so he could contribute to the building of the monastery of San Lorenzo.

El Greco's work shows brilliant color and manipulation of contrast. His work is noteworthy for body elongation, particularly in works such as *Saint Sebastian*. His masterpiece, the *Burial of the Count of Orgaz*, showcases El Greco's Mannerist method of composition.[21]

The Burial of the Count of Orgaz by El Greco.
https://commons.wikimedia.org/wiki/File:El_Greco_-_The_Burial_of_the_Count_of_Orgaz.JPG

[21] Wethey, H. E. (2023, September 23). El Greco. Retrieved from Britannica.com: https://www.britannica.com/biography/El-Greco.

Themes of religious devotion continued into the Baroque period. Philip's successors, notably Philip IV, were major patrons, and the Spanish court was filled with some of Europe's most prominent art patrons. Court portraits were particularly noticeable. The premier painter at the Spanish court was Diego Velázquez.

- Diego Velázquez

Diego Velázquez was a court painter during the reign of Philip IV. His works are a potpourri of commissioned portraits and scenes of everyday life and ordinary people. Velázquez used chiaroscuro, a treatment of light and shadow, in his work. Instead of staying within traditional boundaries, he used naturalism and authenticity in compositions dominated by diagonal structures, complex focal points, and other ways to manipulate the eye. *Las Meninas* is his masterpiece.[22]

Las Meninas by Diego Velázquez.
https://commons.wikimedia.org/wiki/File:Las_Meninas,_by_Diego_Vel%C3%A1zquez,_from_Prado_in_Google_Earth.jpg

---

[22] The Art Story. (2023, October 25). Diego Velazquez. Retrieved from Theartstory.org: https://www.theartstory.org/artist/velazquez-diego/.

There were many other artists who contributed to what can be considered the most significant period of achievement in Spanish art. Bartolomé Esteban Murillo is well known for religious paintings that convey a sense of compassion, tenderness, and piety. His compositions that depicted the Virgin Mary and the Christ child stand out. Francisco de Zurbarán specialized in still-life paintings and displayed a dramatic use of light and shadow with great attention to detail.

Architecture

Imperial Spain was an exporter of artistic innovation, and Spanish colonial architecture in the Philippines and the New World incorporated elements of Spanish Baroque design. While much work was devoted to religious buildings or royal palaces, attention was given to urban planning. Enormous public squares, including the Plaza Mayor, are centers of splendor.

Mudéjar, a blending of Christian and Islamic design elements, was still used by the Spanish Habsburgs. This is interesting because it would not be expected that a family fiercely devoted to the Roman Catholic Church would tolerate any form of Muslim architecture.

An example of architectural coexistence under the Spanish Habsburgs was the Mosque-Cathedral of Córdoba. This Christian cathedral was built in the middle of an enormous Islamic mosque. While Charles V was not impressed by the building, which he saw as a clash of cultures, it must be remembered that another ruler might have ordered the mosque's destruction and built the cathedral on its ruins.

El Escorial

Before the Palace of Versailles was built, there was El Escorial. This complex served as a royal palace, monastery, and burial place for the Spanish monarchs. El Escorial's architectural style is Herrerian, named after the style's principal architect, Juan de Herrera. The scope of El Escorial is massive. There are over 1,200 rooms, and the complex covers 33,000 square meters.

It began to be built in 1563 and was originally intended to be a funerary monument to Charles V, but Philip II decided to expand on the original plans. El Escorial would be both a palace and monastery; a library was later added. It was laid out in a grid plan to emphasize order, balance, clarity, and unity.

Juan de Herrera took over construction management when the first architect died. He believed in severe classicism and drew heavily on the work of Giulio Romano for inspiration. He did not believe in excessive ornamentation. The facade of El Escorial has minimal decoration and focuses on Doric columns to provide a sense of rhythm and structure. The facade is also perfectly symmetrical and uses repetitive elements to enhance a sense of equilibrium.

Precise geometric design is a prominent feature of Herrerian architecture. The complex employs perfect rectangles and squares to create a sense of order. The primary building stone is granite, not marble. It gives a sense of permanence to the structure and a sense of power. That is something the Habsburgs undoubtedly appreciated.[23]

The west façade of El Escorial.
Jebulon, CC0, via Wikimedia Commons;
https://commons.wikimedia.org/wiki/File:Facade_monastery_San_Lorenzo_de_El_Escorial_Spain.jpg

Literature

The Spanish Golden Age also included literary works. The Habsburgs provided financial support and protection to writers, allowing them to devote most of their time to writing. Numerous plays, especially *comedia* (a three-act play with comedic and dramatic elements), sprang

[23] Kilroy-Ewbank, D. L. (2023, October 25). El Escorial, Spain. Retrieved from Khan Academy: https://www.khanacademy.org/humanities/renaissance-reformation/xa6688040:spain-portugal-15th-16th-century/xa6688040:16th-century-spain/a/el-escorial-spain.

from the quills of playwrights like Pedro Calderón de la Barca, Tirso de Molina, and Lope de Vega. The novella took shape during the Habsburg period and would blossom after the Habsburgs left the throne.

Not all the literature written during this period was fiction. Some major works included the writings of Saint Teresa de Jesus, also known as Teresa of Avila, who wrote in the language of mysticism. Her thoughts are still influential in the modern era.

There was one author who stood out from all the writers during the Habsburgs' time on the throne. He delivered what is considered an enduring classic of Western civilization.

A Survivor

We are familiar with those who commanded the fleets during the Battle of Lepanto and some of the lieutenants. The regular soldiers are often faceless in the annals of history. They lived ordinary lives and died forgotten deaths, for the most part, but there was one exception. This man was the son of a surgeon and was wounded on the deck of a Christian warship. His name was Miguel de Cervantes. He is the most famous Spanish author of all time and wrote the classic *Don Quixote.*

There are books and college classes on this remarkable novel, and its interpretations require more space than this book allows. However, we want to bring up one intriguing analysis of Cervantes's work.

The book is a satire that lampoons chivalry and the feudal age. The writing came at a time of significant change in the Iberian Peninsula. The Reconquista had given way to the Age of Discovery, and Spain was at the forefront. Old traditions and customs were falling away, but some people tried to hang on to the traditions. The global economy was being shaped, and men like Hernán Cortés, who would have been nothing more than a freebooter in earlier times, became fabulously wealthy. *Don Quixote* comes at the birth of modern capitalism and implies that the old notions were losing their grip. Greed replaced virtue, and Spain became incredibly rich. The nation had to find new ways to deal with a strange reality.[24]

The Spanish Golden Age would continue for a while longer. The days of glory would eventually fade away, but the cultural contributions

---

[24] Woods, A. (2005, July 19). The 400th Anniversary of Don Quixote: Spain in the Age of Cervantes. Retrieved from Marxist.com: https://www.marxist.com/don-quixote-cervantes150705.htm.

of Spain and the Habsburgs continue to enrich our lives to this day.

Austrian Habsburgs: Northern Renaissance

The Renaissance was much more than Italian paintings and sculpture. Artists were impressed by Italian techniques and incorporated them into their own works. That does not mean that artists from Germany or Flanders only copied the styles of Michelangelo or Titian, though. There was a vibrant Northern Renaissance movement with masters like Hans Holbein and Albrecht Dürer. Their artistic expressions were valuable contributions to the period. The Austrian Habsburgs were significant patrons.

Painting

Art was an essential way of communicating a person's social standing. The aristocracy was just as keen as the royalty was when it came to commissioning and collecting works of art.

Artists were not freelancers in Germany and Austria. They were considered craftsmen and were organized in guilds that had guidelines that needed to be followed. The cities were places where buyers of art could be approached. Albrecht Dürer had no problem selling his prints at local fairs.

The Austrian Habsburgs commissioned artists to paint works for the court. A court appointment was a desired position because it exempted the artist from regulations imposed by a guild. The court artist was expected to paint, stage festivities, and decorate chapels.[25]

Vienna became a cultural center during the Renaissance, and the imperial court attracted numerous artists. Habsburg commissions kept many artists gainfully employed; the rulers wanted artwork for their courts and residences.

Lucas Cranach the Elder worked for the Habsburgs and created portraits such as *Portrait of Emperor Charles V with a Dog*. Giuseppe Arcimboldo worked at the Habsburg court and composed imaginative works that used fruits and vegetables to make faces. *Vertumnus* is an example of his whimsical work. Albrecht Dürer's *Portrait of Maximilian I* is a masterpiece of portraiture.

---

[25] Friehs, J. T. (2023, October 25). Working at Court I: Pro and Contra. Retrieved from The World of the Habsburgs: https://www.habsburger.net/en/chapter/working-court-i-pro-and-contra.

Vertumnus by Arcimboldo depicting Holy Roman Emperor Rudolf II as Vertumnus, the Roman god of seasons.

An artistic giant of the 17ᵗʰ century associated with the Habsburgs was Peter Paul Rubens. This artist was employed by the sovereigns of the Low Countries, Albert VII, Archduke of Austria, and the Infanta Isabella Clara Eugenia of Spain, as their court painter. *The Consequences of War* is one of the paintings Rubens painted for the Habsburgs.

The Consequences of War, also known as The Horrors of War, by Peter Paul Rubens.

Rubens went further than creating portraits. The Spanish Habsburgs used the artist for diplomatic missions and to collect needed information at the royal courts where he worked. Rubens would be both a painter and a diplomat on trips to Spain, England, and the Dutch United Provinces.

The Habsburgs were collectors of art, and their collections displayed incredible pieces. A recent exhibition, "Habsburg Splendor: Masterpieces from Vienna's Imperial Collections," displayed some of the Habsburg artistic possessions. Artists such as Rubens, Tintoretto, Caravaggio, Hans Holbein the Younger, and Velázquez testified to the exquisite taste shown by Habsburg collectors.[26]

Architecture and the Austrian Habsburgs

We typically focus on Michelangelo and Bernini when we think of Renaissance and Baroque architecture. They were great Italian masters, and their styles were extensively copied, but it does not mean that architectural design concepts were only developed in the Italian Peninsula. The Habsburgs played a pivotal role in developing the architecture used in central Europe, and their palaces and imperial residencies show an impressive artistic flair.

The Hofburg was the imperial residence of the Habsburgs and was renovated by Maximilian I, Ferdinand I, and Rudolf II. The religious architecture of the Habsburgs is best exemplified by the restoration of St. Stephen's Cathedral in Vienna.

The Schönbrunn Palace became Habsburg property in 1569 and was originally not much more than a game park. That changed in 1686 when Emperor Leopold II took ownership. Johann Bernhard Fischer von Erlach was assigned the responsibility of designing a palace. Von Erlach's designs planned to make a residence that would rival Versailles and included extensive inclined approaches, elaborate waterworks, and colonnades arranged around a central axis.[27]

---

[26] The Museum of Fine Arts, Houston. (2023, October 25). "Habsburg Splendor: Masterpieces from Vienna's Imperial Collections". Retrieved from MFAH.org: https://www.mfah.org/press/major-traveling-exhibition-masterpieces-austrian-habsburg-dynasty-brings.

[27] Schloss Schonbrunn. (2023, October 25). Architectural History: 17th and 18th Century. Retrieved from Schoenbrunn.at: https://www.schoenbrunn.at/en/about-schoenbrunn/the-palace/history/architectural-history-17th-and-early-18th-century.

The Habsburgs were also interested in creating impressive public buildings. The Spanish Riding School and the Vienna Arsenal are examples of their commitment to architecture. They were willing to draw on the expertise of Italian architects, and the work of Andrea Palladio can be seen in projects commissioned by the imperial family.

Music

France is known for its wine and food, while Italy has a reputation for art. However, Germany and Austria have bragging rights to music, and any musical historian will attest to that. The courts of the Habsburgs hosted composers such as Wolfgang Amadeus Mozart. The Vienna Boys Choir, founded in 1498 by Holy Roman Emperor Maximilian I, is still a world-renowned choral ensemble. Under the Habsburgs, Vienna became a musical hub that welcomed musicians, composers, and other musically inclined professionals.

Maximilian I began the Habsburg family's long association with music when he reorganized his court music in 1498. Vienna became a workshop for musical instruments, notably keyboards and lutes. The Habsburg court chapel became famous for the music it produced. Religious music was very important at the time, and composers employed by the Habsburgs produced motets and masses.[28]

The religious composers produced volumes of sacred music. Cornelius Canis introduced the polyphony style of the Franco-Flemish School to the Habsburg imperial court. His contributions and those of others show sophisticated contrapuntal methods and underscore the Habsburgs' commitment to melody and sound.[29]

The imperial chapels were testing grounds for sacred and secular music in the Baroque period. They were well known for innovation. The Habsburgs encouraged musical education and created music schools and other institutions that served as spawning grounds for talented performers and composers.

Music was used for diplomatic purposes, and the Habsburgs fostered cultural exchanges with other European courts. It is accurate to say that

[28] OAW. (2023, October 25). Music at the Courts of the House of Habsburg. Retrieved from OAW: https://www.oeaw.ac.at/acdh/projects/music-at-the-courts-of-the-house-of-habsburg.

[29] Radioswissclassic. (2023, October 25). Cornelius Canis. Retrieved from Radioswissclassic: https://www.radioswissclassic.ch/en/music-database/musician/54261523c37de6c3eba58ffec69f05ab13193d/biography?app=true.

the Habsburgs founded the laboratories in which the classical music we know and love today was generated.

Science

The Renaissance and the Reformation caused a break with old traditions, and science was where the most significant impact occurred. The Aristotelian and Ptolemaic theories of the heavens came under attack. Copernicus's *De revolutionibus* challenged the old notions of an Earth-centered universe. He believed that the sun, not the Earth, was the focal point of the heavens and that planets revolved around the sun. It was a radical and dangerous notion.

The Roman Catholic Church was committed to the Ptolemaic theory, and it was not alone. The scientific community of the time also embraced Ptolemy. Reputations and careers were built on the false premise of planets revolving around the Earth.

The wrong opinion could have serious consequences for the holder. Galileo Galilei, the leading astronomer of the early 17th century, was forced to recant his belief in the Copernican system. It would take a brave man to challenge the old system. A progressive patron would also be necessary.

Holy Roman Emperor Rudolf II was eccentric. He believed in astrology and was always looking for the philosopher's stone, which could turn base metal into gold. Nevertheless, Rudolf played a dominant role in the scientific inquiry of the 17th century. He had a deep interest in the sciences, and his patronage of prominent scientists and scholars helped advance knowledge. He made his capital, Prague, a center of scientific and intellectual activity, and his support of the sciences made a permanent impression on the development of astronomy, mathematics, and other scientific fields. Rudolph might have seemed a little odd at times, but his support of science was remarkable in an age that still hung on to old beliefs.

Tycho Brahe was an aristocratic astronomer who had a silver nose to replace the one he lost in a duel. He was a Danish citizen and enjoyed the patronage of the king of Denmark, Frederick II (he was not from the House of Habsburg). The observatory he built on Ven Island was famous for its heavenly observations and accuracy of data. Unfortunately, Frederick died in 1588, and his successor, Christian IV, was not very interested in science. The astronomer needed a new patron.[30]

Brahe's international reputation appealed to Rudolf. The Holy Roman emperor officially became Brahe's sponsor in 1599, and the Dane became the imperial court astronomer. Brahe invited a young mathematician named Johannes Kepler in December 1599 to pay a visit. The world of astronomy would never be the same again.

Kepler's visit turned into a permanent relocation to Prague, where he worked for Brahe and was eventually appointed the imperial mathematician. The two had distinct personality differences. Tycho Brahe was a proud and often abrasive aristocrat. Johannes Kepler was a humble person who once aspired to be a Lutheran minister. Despite these differences, both men brought tremendous talents to the table.

Tycho Brahe was famous for his ability to make highly precise and comprehensive astronomical observations. He meticulously recorded the positions of celestial objects, including planets and stars, for many years. Brahe's records were the foundation points for some incredible astronomical conclusions. He also designed astronomical instruments that produced highly accurate data on heavenly positions.

Johannes Kepler was a gifted mathematician who could analyze and synthesize complex astronomical data. His mathematical insights would be instrumental in unraveling the mysteries of planetary motion.

Tycho Brahe proposed a cosmological theory. He believed that the sun and the moon revolved around the Earth and that the other planets went around the sun. It appears he was trying to create a compromise in which the Earth would be recognized as the center of the universe with only two heavenly bodies rotating around it. It made sense politically, but it was questionable scientifically. Brahe's data, which he accumulated over the years, would ultimately prove his theory was wrong.[31]

Brahe died on October 24th, 1601, and Kepler was given the task of completing Brahe's work. Since he had access to the old Dane's statistics, he went to work immediately.

[30] Britannica.com. (2023, October 26). Mature Career of Tycho Brahe. Retrieved from Britannica.com: https://www.britannica.com/biography/Tycho-Brahe-Danish-astronomer/Mature-career.

[31] Redazione. (2018, August 21). Tycho Brahe, Astronomer and Alchemist at the Court of Rudolf II. Retrieved from Progetto: http://www.progetto.cz/tycho-brahe-astronomo-e-alchimista-alla-corte-di-rodolfo-ii/?lang=en.

Profound Discoveries

It is essential to remember that the success Kepler achieved was based on a mountain of data. An opponent would have to argue against the facts. It was accepted wisdom that planetary rotations were circular. Kepler proved that Mars does not make its path around the sun in a perfect circle. He was able to show Mars moved in an elliptical route. Moreover, Mars was at times closer to the sun than at other times, and the planet moved faster when it was farther away.[32]

Armed with the figures of his old mentor, Johannes Kepler's calculations produced three laws of planetary motion:

1. The law of elliptical orbits describes planets moving in elliptical paths with the sun at one of the two foci.

2. The law of equal areas states that a line segment connecting a planet to the sun sweeps out equal areas in equal time intervals.

3. The law of harmonics established a mathematical relationship between a planet's orbital period and its distance from the sun.

The third law demonstrates the beauty of mathematics when it is applied to science. Kepler's work with figures replaced complex and convoluted epicycles with a mathematical harmony that elegantly explained the observed data. One did not have to go into long discourses about how the planets moved and why—just do the math!

The partnership between Tycho Brahe and Johannes Kepler exemplified the power of collaboration in advancing scientific knowledge. Brahe's meticulous observations and innovative instruments provided the empirical foundation, while Kepler's mathematical genius and three laws of planetary motion simplified and explained the complexities of planetary orbits. Together, they ushered in a new era of understanding celestial mechanics, leaving an enduring legacy that transformed the field of astronomy.

The patronage of Rudolf II was instrumental in their success. Brahe and Kepler had the protection of the Holy Roman emperor. The Inquisition would not harass them the way the inquisitors had persecuted Galileo. The two astronomers could pursue truth, and what they discovered was astounding.

---

[32] Famous Scientists. (2023, October 26). Johannes Kepler. Retrieved from Famousscientists.org: https://www.famousscientists.org/johannes-kepler/.

Brahe and Kepler did more than challenge the old order: they proved it was wrong. The two did not do this with philosophical arguments but with meticulous observation and complex mathematics. Critics could not attack their character. Instead, the other side would have to prove the data was flawed. Even so, it would take a while for the old ways to die. Isaac Newton would be the one to drive the last nail in the coffin.

There is an irony in all of this. The Habsburgs were devout Catholics and champions of the church. Brahe and Kepler were Lutherans and would have been in serious trouble under ordinary circumstances. However, Habsburg princes were willing to step outside the box and help astronomers seek the truth. Religious opinions were secondary to scientific achievements.

Rudolf was a great patron of science, but he was a poor politician. He was forced to give up the crown of Bohemia to his brother, Matthias, in 1611. Rudolf died in 1612, and it was fortunate for him. Events were darkening the clouds over central Europe. Germany would soon be tossed into a maelstrom in which nearly a third of the population died.

Chapter 7: Religious Tensions and the Thirty Years' War

The Thirty Years' War devastated Europe from 1618 to 1648 and was rooted deeply in political rivalries, religious tensions, and territorial ambitions. There was a real battle between Protestantism and Catholicism, with the Habsburg dynasty, led by the Holy Roman emperors, positioned as staunch defenders of the Catholic faith. The dynamics of this cataclysm started years before the first shots were fired. The beginning of the end was in the waning days of the 16th century.

The Habsburg Crisis

Spain was the dominant European power in the 16th century. However, cracks were starting to show in the facade. The country was involved in an on-again, off-again war with the Dutch Republic as the Dutch fought for their independence. That was a significant drain on the Spanish treasury. The gold from the New World seemed to be cursed. The bullion was used to finance military campaigns instead of economic growth, and Spain suffered as a result. The reign of Philip III (r. 1598-1621) was a disaster. The Spanish Crown kept accumulating debt until, in 1607, the government was forced to declare a moratorium on its debts.[33]

---

[33] Cavendish, R. (2007, November). Spanish Bankruptcy. Retrieved from History Today: https://www.historytoday.com/archive/spanish-bankruptcy.

The Austrian Habsburgs were not faring much better. The Peace of Augsburg granted some breathing room within the Holy Roman Empire, but it did not mean that hostilities had permanently ended. Calvinism was growing within Germany.

The Calvinists had been an insignificant group when the Peace of Augsburg was initially signed. They were a significant minority in central Europe at the dawn of the 17th century. Prominent rulers in Germany, including the elector of Brandenburg, had declared themselves to be Calvinists. Calvinist activism was disrupting an uneasy peace.

Additionally, there were ecclesiastical principalities within the Holy Roman Empire whose bishops became Protestants. Their refusal to return their lands to the authority of the Roman Catholic Church led to sectarian violence, such as the Cologne War (1583-1588).[34]

Religious Debate

Religion in the late 16th century was highly political. The Protestant Reformation, initiated by Martin Luther in 1517, led to the fragmentation of the Catholic Church's hegemony. Lutheranism and English Anglicanism joined Calvinism as substitutes for Roman Catholicism. This religious diversity ignited tensions between adherents of these reformist faiths and the traditional Catholic establishment.

The Counter-Reformation, spearheaded by the Catholic Church and the Habsburgs, sought to counter the spread of Protestantism. The Council of Trent (1545-1563) implemented reforms within the Catholic Church, emphasizing the importance of doctrine and addressing some of the criticisms raised by the reformers.

Sectarian violence became the standard means of settling disputes. France was wracked by holy wars and atrocities, including the Saint Bartholomew's Day massacre in 1572. The Edict of Nantes ended the violence but granted the Huguenot Protestant minority considerable autonomy. In England, the excommunication of Elizabeth I in 1570 encouraged English Catholics to conspire against her. These secret attempts to overthrow the English monarchy culminated in the Gunpowder Plot of 1605 during the reign of King James I.

---

[34] DailyHistory.org. (2023, October 28). How Did the Peace of Augsburg (1555) Lead to the Thirty Years' War (1618-1648). Retrieved from DailyHistory.org: https://dailyhistory.org/How_did_the_Peace_of_Augsburg_(1555)_lead_to_the_Thirty_Years_War_(1618-1648).

Both Spanish and Austrian Habsburgs made the suppression of Protestants in their respective domains government policy. The Habsburg commitment to Catholicism went beyond the defense of their own territories. They saw themselves as the protectors of the broader Catholic faith and sought to uphold the authority of the pope in Rome.

The Spark That Caused the Fire

The Thirty Years' War started two years before the actual fighting began. Ferdinand Habsburg was crowned Ferdinand II, King of Bohemia, in 1617. Ferdinand was a pious Catholic determined to return Bohemia to the Roman Catholic faith despite many Bohemian nobles being professed Protestants. His efforts to reinstate Catholicism as the official religion of Bohemia and his attempts to curtail the religious freedoms of Protestants in Bohemia and beyond escalated tensions.

Rudolf II signed the Letter of Majesty in July 1609 during his final years as Holy Roman emperor. This letter was a document of religious toleration permitting the various Bohemian Christian denominations to practice their faith peacefully. Rudolf was making good on a promise his father, Holy Roman Emperor Maximilian II, made to the Bohemian estates in 1575. Ferdinand revoked the Letter of Majesty in 1619, enraging the Protestant nobility.[35]

The Defenestration of Prague

The angry nobles refused to allow Ferdinand's act to go unchallenged. The Defenestration of Prague, which occurred on May 23rd, 1618, was the immediate catalyst for the Thirty Years' War. It took place at Prague Castle. Two Catholic officials, Jaroslav Borrzita of Martinice and Count Vilém Slavata, were confronted by Protestant nobles led by Count Jindřich Matyáš Thurn. The Protestants accused the Catholics of violating the religious liberties granted to them by the Letter of Majesty.

The nobles went one step too far. They forcibly ejected Borrzita and Slavata from a window of Prague Castle. Astonishingly, the two men survived the fall, but the event had far-reaching consequences. The Defenestration of Prague became a symbol of Bohemian resistance against Habsburg rule and Catholic influence.[36]

---

[35] The Bohemian Religious Peace (July 1609). (2023, October 28). Retrieved from GHDI: https://ghdi.ghi-dc.org/sub_document.cfm?document_id=4501.

[36] Wilson, D. (2020, May 23). The 1618 Defenestration of Prague Explained. Retrieved from

Yet, there was another even more inflammatory event that led to armed conflict. The Protestants followed up on their demonstration of disapproval by deposing Ferdinand and raising an army of sixteen thousand men. The crown of Bohemia was then offered to Frederick V, Elector of Palatine (his wife was the daughter of James I of England). The rebels had "crossed the Rubicon," and the Thirty Years' War began.

The Defenestration of Prague and Ferdinand II's role in starting the Thirty Years' War exemplify the complex interplay of religious tensions, political ambitions, and dynastic rivalries that defined this conflict. Ferdinand II's unyielding stance on Catholicism and his actions in response to the defenestration set in motion a war that would devastate Europe for three decades. This period of upheaval would ultimately reshape the political and religious landscape of the continent and leave a lasting legacy in European history.

Historians divide this European conflict into four periods: the Bohemian (1618-1625), the Danish (1625-1629), the Swedish (1630-1635), and the French (1635-1648) phases. We will follow these historical classifications.

The Bohemian Phase (1618-1625)

Ferdinand II was not going to accept his deposal graciously. He intended to fight. He was elected Holy Roman emperor on August 28th, 1619, which permitted him to put the military might of the empire on his side in regaining the Bohemian crown. After his election, he immediately started looking for allies. A logical choice for recruiting supporters was the Catholic League.

It was officially called the Catholic League of German States. The Catholic League was a confederation of Catholic princes and states in the Holy Roman Empire. The league was created in response to the Protestant Reformation and the creation of Protestant alliances within Germany. The Catholic League played a significant role in supporting the Habsburgs throughout the war.

The Catholic League gave Ferdinand an army that, by July 1620, had approximately thirty thousand men. Those numbers gave them military superiority over their Protestant enemies, who could only muster ten

History Extra: https://www.historyextra.com/period/stuart/1618-defenestration-prague-facts-history-explained-what-happened-why-castle-protestant-catholic/.

thousand soldiers. Something Ferdinand and his allies had in addition to troop superiority was the military leadership of Johann Tserclaes, Count of Tilly.[37]

Count Johann Tserclaes of Tilly, commonly known as Count Tilly, was a prominent military commander. He played a crucial role in the Bohemian phase of the conflict, particularly in the year 1620. The count began his military career in the Spanish Army and earned his reputation in the wars the Spanish fought against the Dutch. Ferdinand appointed Count Tilly as the commander of the Catholic forces, and he played a primary role in Bohemian campaigns.

Count Tilly's army was different than the usual military forces of the time. It was a standing army whose soldiers did not rely on plunder for pay and provision; the government paid and fed the men. Tilly's advantages against Frederick of Bohemia were more than numbers. Tilly was an experienced commander, and Frederick was not a military man. His inexperience would prove costly.[38]

Battle of White Mountain (November 8th, 1620)

Tilly aggressively took the war to his Protestant enemies. Catholic and Protestant troops met at White Mountain on November 8th, 1620. Tilly's twenty-seven thousand soldiers were disciplined, well trained, and organized into tercios, a highly effective tactical formation used by the Spanish Army. The enemy numbered only fifteen thousand and were mercenaries.

Tilly's forces successfully defeated the less-organized Protestant troops. The battle was a decisive victory for the Catholic Habsburgs, effectively ending Frederick's reign as king of Bohemia.

The Habsburgs held the upper hand after White Mountain, and Ferdinand pressed his advantage with campaigns in Upper Austria and Lower Saxony. Ferdinand consolidated his positions in Germany and moved to restore Catholicism.

Attempting to restore the Catholic Church in Protestant territories might have been a tactical error. Ferdinand could have used his winnings to gain concessions from the Protestant German states, but he failed to

---

[37] New Advent. (2023, October 23). Johannes Tserclaes, County of Tilly. Retrieved from New Advent: https://www.newadvent.org/cathen/14724c.htm.

[38] New Advent. (2023, October 23). Johannes Tserclaes, County of Tilly. Retrieved from New Advent: https://www.newadvent.org/cathen/14724c.htm.

appreciate such an opportunity. Meanwhile, Protestants in Germany were alarmed at the success of the Habsburgs and looked for a way to counter this menacing threat. They found a new champion in the land of the Vikings.

The Danish Phase (1625–1629)

The Danish phase was a critical stage of the war. The defeat of Protestant forces in the Bohemian phase and the subsequent Catholic consolidation of power led to concerns among Protestant leaders throughout the Holy Roman Empire. They saw the need to counter the growing influence of the Catholic Habsburgs.

Scandinavia became Protestant in the early days of the Reformation, and the countries were solidly Lutheran. King Christian IV of Denmark played a central role. Christian sought to lead the Protestant coalition against the Catholic Habsburgs and gain control of critical territories in northern Germany. He entered the conflict not because of any religious conviction but to exploit opportunities that would permit him to enlarge his German territories. He received generous financial support from the Dutch United Provinces and England. The English also sent troops.[39]

Albrecht von Wallenstein

The Habsburgs continued to have the edge when it came to military leadership. The primary Catholic commander during the Danish phase was Albrecht von Wallenstein. He had a reputation for being a brilliant military leader, and he was also able to raise large numbers of men. Ferdinand made him supreme commander of the Catholic forces in the Holy Roman Empire, and von Wallenstein was dispatched to confront the Protestants.

His strategy was different from Tilly's. Wallenstein put his faith in massive mercenary armies. He raised troops anywhere he could find them. He did not care what their religious persuasion was. Many men responded to his recruiting efforts in large numbers because Wallenstein promised the possibility of getting rich from plunder. He was able to recruit and maintain a large army and launch campaigns.

Wallenstein was successful against the Danes. The Danish king used his naval power and was successful in the Baltic Sea, but the land

[39] Infoplease. (2023, October 28). Thirty Years' War: The Danish Period. Retrieved from Infoplease.com: https://www.infoplease.com/encyclopedia/history/modern-europe/wars-battles/thirty-years-war/the-danish-period.

campaigns did not go as well. Wallenstein gained a victory at the Battle of Dessau Bridge (April 25th, 1626) and effectively campaigned against the Protestant leaders Ernst von Mansfeld and Gabriel Bethlen.

It was a bit disturbing that von Wallenstein was more pragmatic than devout. He purchased significant areas of confiscated lands and bought the Duchy of Sagan from Ferdinand. His troops gained a sinister reputation for pillage and plunder. They were guilty of ransacking civilian homes, churches, and business establishments. Brutality and rape were trademarks of his men. Nevertheless, no one could argue with his success. Von Wallenstein's campaigns were fruitful, and his effective leadership achieved the victories that Ferdinand was hoping to achieve.

The Danish phase of the Thirty Years' War ended in 1629 with the Treaty of Lübeck. Christian was permitted to keep all of his pre-war possessions. Still, he had to surrender any claims to Lower Saxon bishoprics, discontinue alliances with North German states, and not interfere with the affairs of the Holy Roman Empire. Denmark received reasonably generous terms, and German Protestants faced rather harsh consequences.

Map of the Thirty Years' War.
*Map_Thirty_Years_War-fr.svg: historicairderivative work: P. S. Burton, CC BY-SA 2.5
<https://creativecommons.org/licenses/by-sa/2.5>, via Wikimedia Commons;
https://commons.wikimedia.org/wiki/File:Map_Thirty_Years_War-en.svg)*

Edict of Restitution

The Danish phase further solidified the power and influence of the Catholic Habsburgs under Emperor Ferdinand II. Their control over the empire was more secure, and Protestant resistance had weakened. Ferdinand issued the Edict of Restitution during the peace negotiations. The terms were tough to swallow.

The Edict of Restitution was a controversial decree. It aimed to restore Catholic lands and properties that had been secularized or confiscated by Protestant rulers since the Peace of Augsburg in 1555. The edict was one of the key measures the Catholic Habsburgs took to reestablish Catholicism and Habsburg authority in the empire.

The Roman Catholic Church was to regain various territories, bishoprics, monasteries, and ecclesiastical properties that had been transferred to Protestant hands in the preceding decades, challenging Protestant gains that had been made over the last few decades.

The edict was to be enforced through imperial commissioners whom Ferdinand appointed. These commissioners were tasked with implementing the terms, often against the will of Protestant rulers. The Protestants hotly contested the stipulations, But what could they do? The Habsburg emperor had them in a corner.[40]

The Danish phase ended in a significant Catholic victory, consolidating Habsburg power within the empire and reinforcing the Edict of Restitution. The German Protestants were routed and understandably demoralized. Fortunately for them, hope and salvation would come from the north.

The Swedish Phase (1630–1635)

The Protestants needed a military genius to beat the Habsburgs, and they got one. Gustavus Adolphus, King of Sweden, was a brilliant military commander and an inspiring leader. He was a match for Count Tilly and von Wallenstein.

Unlike King Christian of Denmark, Gustavus Adolphus was a devout Lutheran who viewed the war as an opportunity to defend the Protestant cause and stop the persecution of the faithful. The king had strategic interests as well, as he hoped to secure territory in northern Germany and spread Swedish influence in the Baltic region. He was the savior the

---

[40] History Learning. (2023, October 28). The Edict of Restitution. Retrieved from History Learning: https://historylearning.com/the-thirty-years-war0/edict-of-restitution/.

Protestants desperately needed. Adolphus stepped on the scene at the right time.

Military Reformer

The military genius of the Swedish king is best demonstrated by the reforms he instituted. Sweden was surrounded by powerful enemies with larger populations, and Adolphus recognized that accepted military practices were not feasible for Sweden.

A significant reform he introduced was universal conscription. Military training was tough, and Adolphus was more inclined to use small mobile units over traditional battlefield formations. The king recognized the importance of firepower and developed effective volley-firing tactics. In addition, he shortened pikes to make them easier to use and had light artillery as opposed to the heavy cannons of the day. Adolphus could use cavalry, artillery, and infantry effectively. These were some reasons why Napoleon Bonaparte considered him one of the most outstanding military leaders in history.[41]

A Lightning Bolt

The Catholic forces were used to winning, and their commanders were probably complacent as the Swedish phase began in 1630. It was a mistake, and the Battle of Breitenfeld (September 17th, 1631) proved that Adolphus could face Count Tilly's troops on the battlefield. The Swedes decisively defeated Tilly. The superiority of the Swedish military system shined that day. Breitenfeld was the first major defeat for the Catholics in the war. It was not going to be the last.

Adolphus moved quickly. He took Nuremberg and captured Munich. He then set his sights on Vienna. Ferdinand brought von Wallenstein back into service, and the mercenary general raised a large force and marched into Saxony. The two armies collided at Lutzen on November 6th, 1632, where Wallenstein was defeated. However, it was a Pyrrhic victory for the Protestants. Adolphus was killed, and the Protestant cause's great hero was gone.

Death of von Wallenstein

Albrecht von Wallenstein was a great general who got too involved in politics. He tried to do some independent peace negotiations and raised

---

[41] Smith, S. S. (2015, August 18). Gustavus Adolphus Revolutionized European Warfare. Retrieved from Investors.com: https://www.investors.com/news/management/leaders-and-success/gustavus-adolphus-father-of-modern-warfare/.

suspicions and questions about his loyalty. Ferdinand was not going to take any chances; he secretly ordered the general killed. What happened on February 25th, 1634, was recorded by Michael Heubel, a tax collector and judge in the 17th century.

"On February 25, by imperial order, Wallenstein, Generalissimus and Duke of Friedland, was murdered together with the counts Terzky und Kinski by a number of officers in Eger, on account of the discovery of high treason on his part, as desired by the king in Hungary Ferdinand III. I saw the room in Eger with two side doors bearing the ineradicable stain of Wallenstein's blood, and also the staircase down which his corpse was dragged feet first, he who only an hour before had been a great duke and is now become the least and most unworthy of all men – so swiftly can the Lord put down the mighty from their seat."[42]

Two of the best military commanders of the Thirty Years' War were now dead.

The Catholics won at Nördlingen in 1634, but a decisive blow was not made. Both sides still had men on the field as the final phase of the Thirty Years' War began.

The French Phase (1635-1648)

The religious sentiments of 1618 were gone by the time the French phase began. This was a period of realpolitik where Catholic France sought to rein in the Catholic Habsburgs.

There was severe competition between France and the Habsburgs for control over Europe. The Bourbons wanted to reduce the power of the Habsburg family. Furthermore, France wanted to gain territorial rights and strategically important territories that would enhance French influence and provide a buffer against Habsburg holdings.

France entered into a series of alliances and agreements with Habsburg enemies. These included Sweden, the Dutch United Provinces, and various German Protestant states. We may think of it as an irony that a Catholic country would unite with Protestants against another Catholic nation. But this is where geopolitics played a more critical role than religion. France wanted to be recognized as a major power, even if it came at the cost of the Catholic Habsburgs.

---

[42] Gruber, S. (2023, October 28). Wallenstein: Death by Murder. Retrieved from The World of the Habsburgs: https://www.habsburger.net/en/chapter/wallenstein-death-murder.

Cardinal Richelieu of France played a significant role. He was the chief minister to King Louis XIII and masterminded France's involvement in the war. The French phase introduced the rest of Europe to the French professional army that had been created. France's military leaders, such as the Vicomte de Turenne, played major roles.

The Battle of Rocroi on May 19th, 1643, was a major battle. It was fought between the Spanish and the French, and it established France as the predominant military power in Europe. The rest of the French phase was primarily a game of chess where diplomatic relations and political intrigue were the main activities.

Peace of Westphalia

Ferdinand II died in 1637. Although this major player in the military drama was now off stage, the fighting still continued. Central Europe was exhausted; there had to be a way out.

The Peace of Westphalia was not one document. Instead, it was a series of peace treaties that were signed between May and October 1648 in the Westphalian cities of Osnabrück and Münster. Besides ending the Thirty Years' War, the treaties also ended the Eighty Years' War that Spain had fought with the Dutch Republic.[43]

Principal Terms of the Peace

- "Cuius regio eius religio" was reestablished.
- Spain officially recognized the sovereignty of the Dutch Republic.
- Sweden and France gained significant territories and emerged as political powers in Europe.
- Various states within the Holy Roman Empire were recognized as being sovereign.
- The Thirty Years' War was officially over.

After decades of confusion and conflict, stability returned to central Europe. The peace and quiet would allow the healing process to begin.

The War's Consequences for Germany

The Thirty Years' War traumatized Germany. Central Europe would not see such devastation until the two world wars of the 20th century.

---

[43] Lumen Learning. (2023, October 28). The Peace of Westphalia and Sovereignty. Retrieved from Lumenlearning.com: https://courses.lumenlearning.com/atd-herkimer-westerncivilization/chapter/the-peace-of-westphalia-and-sovereignty/.

Cities, towns, and the countryside experienced widespread destruction as marauding armies pillaged and destroyed the land. It is a safe estimate that as many as one-third of the population of Germany and central Europe died during this time.

Trade routes were disrupted, agriculture suffered, and many industries were burned to the ground. High levels of taxation increased the people's suffering. There was a legacy of trauma and grief that worked its way into the culture, and the war remained on the minds of people long after the guns were silent.

What was the final result? Neither side actually won. The Protestants and the Catholics gained little, and the old "cuius regio eius religio" returned. The idea of sovereign states grew out of the ashes of the conflict. However, the consequences of the war would remain for years, and Europe had a difficult time recovering.

The Thirty Years' War did not deal a death blow to the Habsburgs, but it did leave them reeling. The Holy Roman Empire was a shell of what it used to be. It was not a significant force anymore. The Spanish and Austrian Habsburgs faced a time of grave troubles. The 18th century would dawn with one branch collapsing while the other fought desperately for its existence.

Chapter 8: The Spanish Succession

The marriage strategy served the Habsburgs well for generations. The family gained thousands of acres of land without spilling blood or drawing a sword. No one suspected the plan would turn sour. However, on November 6th, 1661, things went horribly wrong.

Philip IV of Spain and Mariana of Austria were husband and wife, but they were also uncle and niece. The couple produced a child whom they named Charles. Any geneticist would immediately note that a child from an incestuous marriage would create severe issues. Habsburgs had intermarried before without any trouble, but now the family custom produced a bona fide nightmare. The consequences of successive inbreeding were apparent in Charles.

The boy had a range of both physical and mental deformities. He had a pronounced underbite, a large jaw, and an elongated face—a condition known as the Habsburg jaw or mandibular prognathism. His health issues extended to his mental faculties; he was described as mentally challenged and suffered from developmental delays. His childhood health was precarious, and he suffered from measles, chickenpox, rubella, and smallpox.

Any one of those maladies would have killed an ordinary child, but Charles survived. These infirmities would not have mattered politically if there were other male children in the family, but Charles was the only surviving son of Philip IV. Philip died in 1665 when Charles was only four years old. A child with extreme physical and mental deformities was now the king of Spain.

There were other instances where children were monarchs. Louis XIV is a great example. The problems of the king's incapacities would not have mattered if capable ministers had surrounded Charles II and the succession was clearly defined. There was one challenge, however, that made things worse. Charles married twice during his life and could not produce an heir. In fact, it is possible the king was impotent. It placed the whole matter of succession in turmoil. A lot was riding on who would succeed this invalid.

Portrait of Charles II, c. 1685.
https://commons.wikimedia.org/wiki/File:Juan_de_Miranda_Carreno_002.jpg

The Encircling Game

Spain was not the mega-power it had been one hundred years before, but it was still the largest empire in the world. It held large amounts of territory in the Low Countries and in Italy. A capable successor could govern the empire and be an influential European political figure.

Two major players in European politics had a vested interest in who would succeed Charles. The Austrian Habsburgs had a monopoly on the Holy Roman Empire, but the position of Holy Roman emperor was still elected. The Habsburgs were eager to continue having a hereditary monarchy in Spain to ensure the stability of their power in Europe. By having an Austrian Habsburg holding the Spanish crown, they hoped to further strengthen their position in the Holy Roman Empire. Furthermore, having a Habsburg who had close ties with Vienna and control over the Spanish territories could provide the Austrian Habsburgs with access to vast resources, including gold and silver from the American colonies and strategic territories in Italy, the Low Countries, and other regions. These resources could be used to bolster their military and economic strength. They also needed to checkmate an old rival: France.

France was the premier state in Europe and was ruled by Louis XIV, an ambitious monarch who wanted to enhance the power of his family, the Bourbons. The Austrians saw the Bourbons as a growing threat to the balance of power in Europe. Securing the Spanish crown would allow the Austrian Habsburgs to counterbalance Bourbon power and prevent the emergence of a dominant Bourbon superpower.

Ruling Spain would also prevent the Austrian Habsburgs from becoming encircled. If the Bourbons controlled both France and Spain, the Austrian Habsburgs would be geographically surrounded by Bourbon territories, which could potentially isolate and weaken their position in Europe.

Interestingly, the Habsburgs' worries were also the Bourbons' concerns. The Bourbons were motivated by a desire to prevent the Austrian Habsburgs from gaining control of the Spanish crown. Allowing the Habsburgs to hold both Spain and the Holy Roman Empire could create a formidable Habsburg superpower that might threaten the interests of the Bourbon dynasty and its allies. Conversely, the Bourbons understood that securing the Spanish throne would allow them to exert influence over critical regions, such as Italy and the Low Countries, and potentially shift the balance of power in Europe in their favor.

Two Claimants

Contested European successions often resulted in a mad dash to the genealogical tables to discover who had the best claim to an open throne by means of bloodline. The French claimant, Philip of Anjou, claimed his right from his connection to Anne of Austria, Philip IV's older sister, and Maria Theresa, Philip's eldest daughter. The Austrian claimant,

Charles, Archduke of Austria, argued that the right of succession was based on his grandmother, Maria Anna, who was the youngest daughter of Philip IV. Philip of Anjou was the grandson of Louis XIV, and Charles was the son of Holy Roman Emperor Leopold I.

The Bourbon claim to the throne was stronger, and Louis XIV schemed to make a Bourbon succession a reality. He signed two separate treaties with William III of England to divide the Spanish Empire in 1698 and 1700 but forgot to ask Charles II what he thought about the arrangements. Charles might have been less than brilliant, but the Spanish king was adamant about keeping the empire intact.[44]

Emerging Alliances

Charles II of Spain was growing physically weaker, and he died on November 1st, 1700. He left behind a will that named Philip of Anjou as his successor. That should have been the end of the story, but it was not.[45]

England and the Dutch Republic were concerned that a Bourbon king on the throne of Spain would create a Bourbon superpower. They wanted to prevent the Bourbons from upsetting the balance of power in the continent. The Grand Alliance was formed in 1701 and included the Holy Roman Empire, England, and the Dutch Republic.

France was also looking for allies to back the Bourbon candidate. The French renewed their alliance with Spain and added Bavaria as an ally to protect the nation's southern front from war.

Other alliances would be formed in the following years. All of these illustrate the intricate diplomatic maneuverings that took place. Both sides were willing to fight, and all that remained were formal declarations of war. Hostilities began in March 1701 when the French seized Spanish fortresses in the Spanish Netherlands.

The Greatest Habsburg General

Some historians believe that the War of the Spanish Succession was the first world war of the modern era. The Grand Alliance was determined to thwart the French. The Grand Alliance was fortunate to

[44] Lumen Learning. (2023, October 28). War of Spanish Succession. Retrieved from Lumenlearning.com: https://courses.lumenlearning.com/suny-fmcc-boundless-worldhistory/chapter/war-of-spanish-succession/.
[45] Britannica.com. (2023, October 28). War of the Spanish Succession. Retrieved from Britannica.com: https://www.britannica.com/event/War-of-the-Spanish-Succession.

have two of the best military commanders of the 18th century: John Churchill, Duke of Marlborough, and Prince Eugene of Savoy. We know much about the Duke of Marlborough thanks to the writings of his descendant, Winston Churchill. Prince Eugene sometimes gets pushed into the background. That is unfortunate because the short military commander was one of the best generals in Austrian history.

It is ironic that he fought against the French because Prince Eugene was the son of French aristocrats. He was supposed to follow a career in the church, but as a young man, he balked at the idea. He wanted to join the French military, but King Louis XIV blocked his career path. That did not stop the young man. He went to Vienna, where he received a commission in the Austrian army and helped raise the siege of Vienna in 1688.

Prince Eugene was highly successful as a military officer and rose rapidly through the ranks. He played a primary role in driving the Ottomans out of Hungary and was a field marshal when the War of Spanish Succession broke out.[46]

Most military officers at the time gained their positions because of their family connections. Prince Eugene, on the other hand, did it through sheer talent. He had a keen understanding of warfare and had the ability to adapt to different battlefield conditions. Eugene displayed remarkable versatility by excelling in both offensive and defensive operations. He had a wide range of military skills and was equally adept at commanding cavalry charges and infantry engagements. One talent he had that is sometimes overlooked was his ability to work effectively with other military commanders. His relationship with the Duke of Marlborough was a stellar example of his flexibility.

---

[46] Visiting Vienna. (2023, June 7). Prince Eugene: What You Need to Know. Retrieved from Visitingvienna.com: https://www.visitingvienna.com/culture/prince-eugene-savoy/.

Prince Eugene of Savoy.
https://commons.wikimedia.org/wiki/File:Prinz_Eugene_of_Savoy.PNG

A Splendid Partnership

The partnership between the Duke of Marlborough (John Churchill) and Prince Eugene of Savoy during the War of the Spanish Succession is often regarded as one of the most successful and effective military collaborations in European history. Their alliance played a pivotal role in achieving significant victories for the Grand Alliance against the forces of France and Bavaria. It was an amazing alignment of two martial stars that delivered substantial victories. There were some key ingredients to their success.

Marlborough and Eugene possessed complementary military strengths. Marlborough was known for his strategic acumen, ability to formulate grand plans, and strong leadership qualities. Eugene, on the other hand, excelled at tactical warfare, displaying remarkable skills in maneuvering troops on the battlefield and making crucial decisions in the heat of battle. Together, they formed a balanced and effective leadership team.

Both men were united by a common purpose: to defeat the forces of France and Bavaria. Their shared commitment to this overarching goal allowed for cooperation and strategic alignment. Marlborough and Eugene developed comprehensive strategic plans that emphasized joint operations. They carefully planned their campaigns and ensured that their forces moved in harmony, preventing the enemy from dividing and conquering them.

They made vital decisions jointly, consulting with each other and seeking consensus. Their partnership was not characterized by rivalry or ego-driven decision-making but rather by a commitment to making choices that would best serve the interests of the Grand Alliance.

The two were flexible. They were open to adapting their plans and strategies based on changing battlefield conditions and enemy movements. This adaptability allowed them to respond effectively to unexpected challenges.

The pair also had mutual respect for each other. They recognized each other's strengths and were willing to defer to the expertise of the other when necessary. This mutual respect formed the basis of their strong working relationship.

They knew how to communicate as well. Despite lingual differences (Marlborough spoke English, while Eugene spoke primarily French and German), they maintained clear lines of communication and exchanged regular correspondence to coordinate their military actions.

All of these qualities would pay off handsomely in the single most crucial battle of the war: the Battle of Blenheim.

The Battle of Blenheim

Military historians count Blenheim as one of the fifteen decisive battles in world history. A French army of sixty thousand men was put against the Grand Alliance army's approximately fifty-six thousand men.

The early days of the war were fought primarily in the Low Countries, but the French, in 1704, decided to take the offensive against Austria with the intention of destroying the Austrian Habsburgs. The Duke of Marlborough was the commander in chief of the Grand Alliance forces, and he marched his army to counter the French in southern Germany.[47]

---

[47] BritishBattles.com. (2023, October 28). Battle of Blenheim. Retrieved from BritishBattles.com: https://www.britishbattles.com/war-of-the-spanish-succession/battle-of-blenheim/.

Marlborough coordinated his movements with Prince Eugene, and Marlborough led his troops on a crossing of the Danube near Donauwörth on July 31ˢᵗ, 1704. This enabled him to join up with Eugene and position their army against the French soldiers under Marshal Tallard and the Bavarian forces commanded by Maximilian of Bavaria.

The French did not expect Marlborough and Eugene to attack. They should have. The forces of the Grand Alliance moved forward on August 13ᵗʰ, 1704, and concentrated on the French center. The battle saw intense fighting, including artillery bombardments and infantry clashes. Tallard's forces initially held their ground, but as the battle progressed, their position weakened.

A decisive moment occurred when Marlborough launched an aggressive cavalry attack on the French center, leading to the collapse of the enemy lines. Marshal Tallard was captured, and Maximilian fled the battlefield. The Battle of Blenheim resulted in a resounding victory for the Grand Alliance.

The myth of French superiority was crushed. The Battle of Blenheim marked a turning point in the War of the Spanish Succession. It halted French expansion into the heart of the Holy Roman Empire and bolstered the morale of the Grand Alliance. It furthermore demonstrated the brilliance of Marlborough and Eugene working together as a team.

A String of Magnificent Victories

After the resounding victory at the Battle of Blenheim in 1704, the partnership between the Duke of Marlborough and Prince Eugene of Savoy continued to yield significant achievements for the Grand Alliance. Their combined military leadership and strategic coordination led to a series of triumphs that further weakened the Bourbon position in the war.

• Battle of Ramillies (May 23ʳᵈ, 1706)

The Grand Alliance achieved a decisive victory over the French and Bavarian forces under Marshal Villeroy. The battle resulted in the capture of a significant portion of the French Army and allowed the alliance to regain control of the Spanish Netherlands.

• Capture of Brussels (June 6ᵗʰ, 1706)

Marlborough and Eugene advanced into the Spanish Netherlands and captured the city of Brussels, a key strategic stronghold. This success further solidified their control over the region.

- Siege of Lille (August 12th–December 10th, 1708)

Marlborough and Eugene jointly conducted the siege of Lille, which was a prominent French stronghold. The siege resulted in the surrender of the city to the Grand Alliance forces and the capture of a substantial French garrison. The fall of Lille was a significant blow to French military capabilities.

- Battle of Oudenaarde (July 11th, 1708)

Marlborough and Eugene defeated the French and Bavarian forces commanded by Marshal Vendôme. The victory prevented a French attempt to relieve the besieged city of Lille and further secured the Grand Alliance's control over the Spanish Netherlands.

- Battle of Malplaquet (September 11th, 1709)

The Battle of Malplaquet was one of the bloodiest engagements of the war, with heavy casualties on both sides. Although the French and Bavarians under Marshal Villars put up a strong defense, Marlborough and Eugene eventually achieved victory. Malplaquet reinforced the Grand Alliance's position and contributed to their continued control over the Spanish Netherlands.

These victories, achieved through the joint leadership of Marlborough and Eugene, significantly weakened the French-Bavarian alliance and expanded the territory controlled by the Grand Alliance. The military successes of Marlborough and Eugene played a crucial role in advancing the interests of the Habsburg monarchy and the broader Grand Alliance during the War of the Spanish Succession.

Politics Intervene

The French were losing on the battlefield, but it did not mean they would lose the war. Politics played a dominating role in the final years of the war.

In 1711, Holy Roman Emperor Joseph I died. He was succeeded by Archduke Charles, which created a conundrum for the Grand Alliance. Charles would not only be the Holy Roman emperor but also the king of Spain, creating a powerful position for the Habsburgs that had not been seen since the 16th century. It would be a severe shift in the balance of power.[48]

Both sides began to maneuver and secretly negotiate for peace terms. The English and French signed the Preliminary Articles of London on October 8th, 1711. France agreed that the Spanish and French crowns would remain separate, and Great Britain was given a thirty-year monopoly on the right to import enslaved people into Spanish American colonies. Other peace negotiations occurred that involved multiple parties, but everyone wanted an end to the conflict.

Finally, two peace agreements were hammered out.

Treaty of Utrecht and Treaty of Rastatt

The principal peace agreement was the Treaty of Utrecht. Its main provisions were the following:

- Recognition of Philip V: The treaty recognized Philip V, the Bourbon claimant, as the legitimate king of Spain with the condition that the French and Spanish crowns would remain separate.
- Territorial changes: Significant territorial adjustments were made in Europe and overseas. Spain ceded several territories to other European powers, including the Spanish Netherlands, Naples, Sardinia, and parts of Milan to the Austrian Habsburgs and Sicily to the Duchy of Savoy. Gibraltar and Minorca were ceded to Great Britain. France ceded Newfoundland, Nova Scotia, and Rupert's Land to Great Britain.

The Treaty of Utrecht was signed on April 11th, 1713, between the major European powers.

The Treaty of Rastatt was a complementary agreement to the Treaty of Utrecht. It confirmed many of the territorial changes outlined in the Treaty of Utrecht, and it addressed issues related to the Holy Roman Empire, including the transfer of certain territories from Spain to the Holy Roman Empire. The Treaty of Rastatt was signed on March 7th, 1714, between the Holy Roman Empire and France.

---

[48] The Royal Hampshire Regiment. (2023, October 28). The War of the Spanish Succession. Retrieved from Royalhampshirereiment.org: https://www.royalhampshireregiment.org/about-the-museum/timeline/war-spanish-succession/.

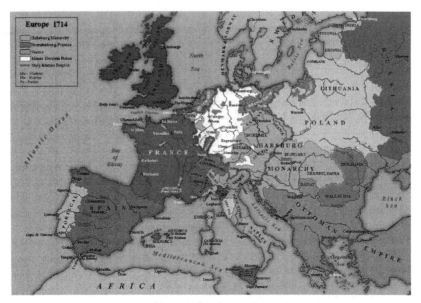

Europe after the treaties.

https://commons.wikimedia.org/wiki/File:Europe,_1714.png

Pragmatic Sanction of 1713

Concurrently with the peace negotiations, Emperor Charles VI of the Holy Roman Empire sought to secure the Pragmatic Sanction of 1713, which ensured the inheritance of the Habsburg lands by a daughter instead of only a son. The European powers agreed to this arrangement as part of the broader settlement.

These treaties helped establish a more stable and peaceful order in Europe, although they also left lingering tensions and rivalries that would influence later conflicts. The Habsburgs did not get all they wanted, but the acquisition of the Spanish Netherlands gave Austria increased tax revenues. While the Spanish Habsburg line was no more, the Austrian Habsburgs were as powerful as they ever had been.

Chapter 9: The Reign of Maria Theresa

The end of the War of the Spanish Succession saw the Habsburgs lose one crown and risk losing another. Holy Roman Emperor Charles VI did not have a male heir, and it was quite possible that someone outside of the family would become the ruler of the Holy Roman Empire. It was another succession crisis, and the Habsburgs had to win this one or lose all its imperial power.

The Pragmatic Sanction of 1713 outlined the succession after his death. A critical clause in the document was that the eldest daughter of Charles, Maria Theresa, was in the direct line of succession to the throne. Charles spent the last years of his life getting the major European powers to recognize the Pragmatic Sanction. He succeeded in his lifetime, but his succession plan was immediately contested after he died. Albert of Bavaria and Frederick the Great of Prussia both contested the succession. Neither counted on the charisma and courage of a young woman determined to obey her father's wishes.

Queen Elizabeth I of England rallied her troops at Tilbury by saying, "I know I have but the body of a weak and feeble woman, but I have the heart and stomach of a king, and of a king of England too."[49] That

---

[49] Royal Museums Greenwich. (2023, November 8). Queen Elizabeth I's Speech to the Troops at Tilbury. Retrieved from Rmg.co.uk: https://www.rmg.co.uk/stories/topics/queen-elizabeth-speech-troops-tilbury.

description fits Maria Theresa. She was not inclined to go quietly into the dark shadows of history. Maria Theresa was willing to put up a fight even if her chances appeared slim.

The State of War

Maria Theresa ascended the throne on October 20th, 1740. She was barely settled into her new title when Frederick the Great sent the Prussian army into Silesia on December 16th, 1740. He was not alone in his attack on Habsburg territory. France and Bavaria also took advantage of the situation and launched invasions of Austrian territory. Eventually, Maria Theresa faced an alliance of France, Bavaria, Spain, Sweden, and Saxony, even though several of the members of this alliance had agreed to the Pragmatic Sanction. They saw an opportunity to expand their territory at the expense of the new monarch.[50]

Maria Theresa desperately needed the help of the Hungarian aristocracy if she wanted to protect her crown successfully. She decided to convene a meeting of the Hungarian Diet in Bratislava to make a personal appeal.

The empress traveled to Bratislava to beg for help. There is a legend regarding what she did that convinced the Hungarians to rally for her cause. She faced opposition because she was a woman. To overcome any question of her abilities, Maria Theresa reputedly rode a horse up the steep steps of St. Martin's Cathedral in Bratislava to display her determination and commitment to the Hungarian cause. This act was intended to win the Hungarian nobles' admiration and support. She went further by pleading with the assembled nobles dressed in Hungarian-style clothing and with her infant son in her arms. It is said that the Hungarian nobles were so moved that a general cry of "We will die for our queen, Maria Theresa!" rose up as the Hungarian nobles swore to give their assistance to the embattled monarch.[51]

Whether the legend is true is a topic for debate. Regardless, Maria Theresa made a formal promise to uphold the rights and privileges of the Hungarian nobility, including their traditional liberties and the autonomy of the Kingdom of Hungary within the Habsburg Empire.

---

[50] Biography.com. (2021, October 21). Maria Theresa. Retrieved from Biography.com: https://www.biography.com/royalty/maria-theresa.

[51] History's Women. (2023, November 8). Maria Theresa. Retrieved from History's Women: https://historyswomen.com/women-who-ruled/maria-theresa/.

This promise was known as her "Hungarian Pragmatic Sanction."

Maria Theresa's willingness to engage directly with the Hungarian nobility and make concessions to preserve their traditional rights earned her their loyalty and admiration. The aristocracy saw her as a ruler who respected their privileges and traditions. Her bold initiative resulted in her coronation as queen of Hungary in St. Martin's Cathedral on June 25th, 1741.

The War of the Austrian Succession plodded on for years. Maria Theresa refused the offer made by Frederick the Great to end the war in return for recognition of Prussian control of Silesia and continued the fight. She had the support of Great Britain but was forced to concede Silesia to Prussia in the Treaty of Dresden, which was signed in December 1745.

The war finally grounded to a halt and was ended by the Treaty of Aix-la-Chapelle, signed on October 18th, 1748. Austria formally gave up Silesia and surrendered the duchies of Parma, Piacenza, and Guastalla in Italy to Spain. Nevertheless, the treaty formalized the succession of Maria Theresa to the Habsburg holdings in Austria. Her throne was secure.

A portrait of Maria Theresa.
https://commons.wikimedia.org/wiki/File:Kaiserin_Maria_Theresia_(HRR).jpg

It did not end Austria's involvement in future European wars. Maria Theresa later led her empire into the Seven Years' War and the War of Bavarian Succession.

The Habsburg Reformer

Because Maria Theresa was now Austria's recognized ruler, she could concentrate on a series of reforms to modernize her country. She was a conservative ruler but was open to changes that would improve the administration of her domains and the living conditions of her subjects. Maria Theresa compiled an impressive record of reforms. These changes touched upon various aspects of governance, administration, education, the military, and the economy.

Administrative Reforms

Maria Theresa centralized the administration of her extensive domains, which included the Holy Roman Empire and other territories. Her administrative reforms aimed to streamline the bureaucracy, make it more efficient, and promote uniform governance across her realms. Critical aspects of her administrative reforms included the following:

- Creation of provincial councils: Maria Theresa established provincial councils in different regions to improve local administration. These councils were responsible for various administrative functions and helped in the collection of taxes and the maintenance of law and order.
- Codification of laws: She undertook efforts to codify and standardize laws in her territories. The Codex Theresianus, a comprehensive legal code, was promulgated in 1766, simplifying legal procedures and providing greater legal clarity.

Educational and Cultural Reforms

Maria Theresa was a staunch supporter of education and culture. Her reforms aimed to promote knowledge and intellectual development. Some of her notable initiatives included:

- Founding Theresianum: In 1746, Maria Theresa founded Theresianum, a prestigious educational institution in Vienna. It served as a model school and academy and trained students for careers in public service.
- Expansion of schools and universities: Maria Theresa promoted the establishment of schools and universities in her realms, These institutions contributed to the spread of education and knowledge. Maria Theresa introduced

compulsory schooling for children in all Habsburg hereditary lands in 1774. This was the beginning of mandatory education for large segments of the population.

Military Reforms

Austria's armed forces were out-generaled and out-maneuvered by Prussia in the War of the Austrian Succession. Maria Theresa knew changes were going to be needed.

- Professionalization of the army: She professionalized the Habsburg army by introducing standardized training, uniforms, and discipline. This modernization improved the efficiency and effectiveness of the military.

Economic Reforms

Economic stability and growth were high priorities for Maria Theresa. Her economic reforms aimed to promote trade, support agriculture, and stimulate industry. The following sums up her economic reforms:

- Mercantilist policies: She implemented mercantilist policies to boost domestic production and trade. These policies included tariffs, subsidies, and regulations designed to protect and nurture domestic industries.
- Agricultural reforms: Maria Theresa encouraged improvements in agriculture through land reforms and incentives for landowners to adopt more productive farming techniques, which contributed to increased agricultural output.
- Infrastructure development: She invested in infrastructure development, including the construction of roads and canals, to facilitate trade and transportation within her realms.[52]

Maria Theresa's reforms significantly modernized her realms and promoted their development. While not all of her reforms were universally successful, her reign left a lasting impact on the Habsburg monarchy and the broader European landscape, contributing to its stability and progress during the 18th century.

Diplomatic Revolution of 1756

The Diplomatic Revolution of 1756 was a significant realignment of European alliances that took place in the mid-18th century. It marked a

[52] Gruber, S. (2023, November 8). *Maria Theresa: The "Great Reformer."* Retrieved from The World of the Habsburgs: https://www.habsburger.net/en/chapter/maria-theresa-great-reformer.

dramatic shift in the balance of power and geopolitical relationships among major European states. The key feature of this diplomatic transformation was the reversal of longstanding alliances and the formation of new partnerships. The Diplomatic Revolution was a response to changing European political, territorial, and strategic considerations.

Maria Theresa of Austria played a pivotal role in the Diplomatic Revolution of 1756. Her diplomatic efforts during this period were aimed at countering the growing power of Prussia and safeguarding the interests of the Habsburg monarchy.

Maria Theresa was a skilled diplomat, and several notable diplomatic accomplishments marked her reign. Among her most significant achievements was the appointment of Wenzel Anton, commonly known as Count Kaunitz, as her chief diplomat and chancellor.

Kaunitz was one of the most influential diplomats and statesmen during Maria Theresa's reign. He played a pivotal role in shaping Maria Theresa's foreign policy and contributing to her diplomatic successes. Kaunitz played a central role in the Diplomatic Revolution of 1756. His most notable diplomatic achievement was the role he played in creating an alliance with France.

A portrait of Kaunitz.

It was an audacious move. France and Austria had been enemies for centuries, and the friendship agreement that Kaunitz was able to create showed how realpolitik was shaping European diplomacy. France was upset with an alliance Prussia entered into with Great Britain, and the French needed something to counterbalance that relationship. Kaunitz and Maria Theresa saw an opportunity to make a move against Prussia, and the two decided to ignore the age-old differences between France and Austria.

Negotiations led to the Treaty of Versailles on May 1st, 1756, and then another Treaty of Versailles, signed on May 1st, 1757. France and Austria became allies against Prussia, agreeing to fight against Frederick the Great until Austria regained control of Silesia and Glantz.[53]

While the Diplomatic Revolution did not result in an immediate resolution to European conflicts such as the Seven Years' War, it laid the foundation for the broader realignment of alliances in Europe and contributed to a more complex and multipolar system of power in the continent.

Maria Theresa's decision to ally with France was a diplomatic masterstroke. It signaled her commitment to curbing Prussian expansionism and allowed her to secure critical French support in the event of future conflicts. A treaty signed with Russia at approximately the same time solidified Austria's position in central Europe.

Maria Theresa's diplomatic skills and willingness to form alliances with former adversaries demonstrated her ability to adapt to changing circumstances and prioritize the interests of the Habsburg monarchy.

The Partition of Poland

Austria was involved in the Seven Years' War because it hoped to regain Silesia. The Treaty of Hubertusburg in 1763 ended Austria's involvement in the Seven Years' War. Austria gained some diplomatic successes and regained lost territories, but Silesia was permanently lost. However, Austria later gained some significant regions in Europe at the expense of a neighboring state.

The partition of Poland, one of the most significant events in European history during the late 18th century, involved the division and eventual dismemberment of the Polish-Lithuanian Commonwealth, a

---

[53] New Advent. (2023, November 8). *Wenzel Anton Kaunitz.* Retrieved from NewAdvent.org: https://www.newadvent.org/cathen/08611b.htm.

once-powerful state in central and eastern Europe. This partition occurred in three stages, with the participation of several European powers, including Austria.

Poland's government was inherently weak and was torn apart in the late 1760s by a civil war. Poland lacked the political will to resist the pressures exerted on it by Russia and had no support from other European powers. Russia, Prussia, and Austria signed a treaty that partitioned Poland on August 5th, 1772.

As audacious as this blatant land grab was, the Polish Sejm, the country's governing body, ratified the partition on September 30th, 1773. Poland lost nearly half its population and roughly one-third of its landmass. Austria acquired Galicia and Lodomeria (a region in present-day Ukraine and Poland) as its share of the partition.[54]

Austria participated in the partition of Poland to expand its territory and influence in eastern Europe. Maria Theresa acquired Polish territories that were rich in resources and had strategic significance. Moreover, Austria was concerned about the growing dominance of Russia and Prussia in the region. The partition permitted Austria to counterbalance the influence of those two states and prevent either from gaining more power in eastern Europe.

Maria Theresa and the Age of Enlightenment

The Age of Enlightenment was a period marked by intellectual, cultural, and political transformations. Maria Theresa's role during the Enlightenment was complex and multifaceted.

While Maria Theresa implemented some Enlightenment-inspired reforms, she was not immune to criticism from Enlightenment thinkers who called for more radical changes. Some of her policies were conservative, and she maintained a strong central authority.

A combination of reformist policies, cultural patronage, and a degree of openness to Enlightenment ideas marked Maria Theresa's contributions to the Age of Enlightenment. Her reign reflected a balance between the desire for centralized authority and the recognition of the need for modernization and improvement in governance. She abolished torture, limited the judicial authority of landlords over serfs, and removed universities from the control of the Roman Catholic Church.

---

[54] Britannica.com. (2023, October 17). *Partitions of Poland.* Retrieved from Britannica.com: https://www.britannica.com/event/Partitions-of-Poland.

Her agrarian reforms were founded on fiscal and humanitarian reasons. She did not go as far as some reformers hoped, but the changes Maria Theresa instituted had lasting positive effects.[55]

A Patron of the Arts

Maria Theresa made significant cultural contributions during her rule. Her patronage of the arts played a pivotal role in shaping the cultural landscape of the Habsburg monarchy during the 18th century. She was particularly fond of music and opera. Maria Theresa supported the Viennese court's musical life and was known to attend performances regularly. She helped court composers like Joseph Haydn, who served in her court. Haydn's music and compositions contributed significantly to the Classical period of music. Maria Theresa also patronized renowned artists, including painters like Martin van Meytens.[56]

Culture was incorporated into Maria Theresa's diplomatic efforts as well. She exchanged gifts and artistic treasures with other European courts. These exchanges fostered cultural ties and promoted the Habsburg monarchy's prestige.

Maria Theresa's patronage and support of the arts made Vienna a major European cultural center. She left a lasting legacy that enriched the cultural heritage of the Habsburg realm and contributed to the broader cultural developments of the 18th century.

Maria Theresa died on November 29th, 1780. Her reign was marked by significant accomplishments in various fields, including governance, administration, culture, and diplomacy. Her ability to navigate the challenges of her time and leave a lasting legacy makes her one of the most notable rulers in European history. Historians consider her one of the most important Habsburg rulers.

---

[55] Keithly, D. M. (2008, April 3). *Maria Theresa.* Retrieved from Enlightenment-revolution.org: https://enlightenment-revolution.org/index.php?title=Maria_Theresa.

[56] History's Women. (2023, November 8). Maria Theresa. Retrieved from History's Women: https://historyswomen.com/women-who-ruled/maria-theresa/.

Chapter 10: The Napoleonic Era and the Age of Metternich

Maria Theresa was succeeded by her son Joseph II, who also instituted reforms to improve government and society. His younger brother, Leopold II, followed him; his reign lasted only two years.

Austria was involved in a war against the Turks during the reign of both monarchs. That conflict, which was part of a treaty obligation to assist the Russians, was the last Austro-Turkish war. It was finally concluded by the signing of the Treaty of Sistova in 1791.

Unfortunately, Leopold permitted the cancellation of many of his older brother's reforms and increased the power of the secret police. Perhaps what influenced the end of those progressive reforms could have been a response to what was happening in France.

The French Revolution broke out in 1789 and severely attacked the old order. Francis II (later Francis I of Austria), who succeeded Leopold II, opposed the French Revolution and the treatment of France's king, Louis XVI. Relations between the two allies grew strained to the point where the French declared war on Austria in April 1792, beginning a series of conflicts that would wrack Europe for the next twenty-three years.[57]

---

[57] Britannica.com. (2023, November 8). Conflicts with Revolutionary France, 1790-1805. Retrieved from Britannica.com: https://www.britannica.com/place/Austria/Conflicts-with-revolutionary-France-1790-1805.

Sheer Military Incompetence

Austria fought five wars with France during this troubled period and lost four of them. Austria was a key player in the War of the First Coalition (1792-1797), forming alliances with other European monarchies to counteract the revolutionary French forces. The empire had initial successes but quickly stumbled against the French and began to lose consistently.

Fighting the French in Italy was a total disaster. Austria had the misfortune of dealing with a military genius named Napoleon Bonaparte. Napoleon led a highly skilled, disciplined army. The French troops were well trained and experienced; they clearly understood Napoleon's innovative tactics. The Battle of Marengo in 1800 is a prime example of this. The Austrian army's inability to adapt to the rapidly changing battlefield conditions contributed to its defeat. Austria faced resource limitations, including difficulties maintaining and supplying its troops in Italy. The financial and logistical strain of sustaining a campaign in Italy placed additional burdens on the Habsburg monarchy.

The Austrian army was large but suffered from rigidity, worn-out strategies, and obsolete battle tactics. There were highly competent commanders, such as Archduke Charles (son of Emperor Leopold II), but there were also instances of less capable leadership. Austria's officers were often appointed based on social status rather than merit, and many were inexperienced or incompetent.

Austria's army relied on linear formations and slow maneuvers. The French, on the other hand, were using modern innovations, such as moving troops in column formations and the corps system. Poor leadership at Rivoli in 1797 was the reason for the Austrian defeat.

Napoleon consistently out-maneuvered and out-fought the Austrians in Italy. The consequence of the poor Austrian performance was the Treaty of Campo Formio in 1797. Austria was forced to cede Lombardy to France.

Lombardy's loss was a significant blow to Austria's influence in Italy. This territory became part of the Cisalpine Republic, a French client state. Austria was required to recognize the Cisalpine Republic and the Ligurian Republic. Austria also gave up the Austrian Netherlands and recognized the French annexation of the left bank of the Rhine.

Some consequences harmed Austria years after the guns fell silent. The French occupation of Italian territory exposed the local population to the revolutionary ideals of liberty, equality, and nationalism. Those ideas had a lasting impact on the Italian Peninsula, contributing to the emergence of nationalist sentiments and movements that would shape the course of Italian unification in the 19th century.

Map of central Europe after the Treaty of Campo Formio.
https://commons.wikimedia.org/wiki/File:Peace_of_Basel.png

<u>Third Coalition Disaster</u>

The Third Coalition was a military alliance formed in 1805 to respond to the expanding ambitions of Napoleon Bonaparte and the French Republic during the Napoleonic Wars. The expanding ambitions of Napoleon Bonaparte prompted this alliance. Its member nations were Austria, Great Britain, Russia, Naples, Sweden, and Sicily. Archduke Charles was a principal commander of the Third Coalition forces.

Austria attacked Bavaria, France's ally, on September 10th, 1805. Napoleon responded by marching into central Europe. The Third Coalition was confident of victory since the Russians and Austrians who confronted the French outnumbered the French two to one.

Napoleon moved rapidly and surprised Austrian General Karl Mack von Leiberich at Ulm on October 19th. The Austrians suffered a horrific defeat, losing almost all of Mack's army. The road was now opened for the French to march on Vienna. As Francis fled his capital, Napoleon entered Vienna on November 14th, 1805. The Third Coalition still had an army in the field, and Napoleon moved against it.[58]

The French emperor understood the intentions of the coalition forces and initiated a series of rapid and daring maneuvers. He feigned weakness, enticing the coalition to pursue him while he concentrated on his forces. He chose a battlefield at Austerlitz that offered significant advantages. The terrain included a gently sloping plateau known as the Pratzen Heights advantage.

The Battle of Austerlitz commenced on December 2nd, 1805. The coalition forces launched attacks on the French center, which Napoleon had deliberately weakened. The French right and left wings executed a well-coordinated counterattack, driving a wedge between the Russo-Austrian forces and isolating their left wing on the Pratzen Heights. Napoleon, using brilliant strategy and execution, destroyed the coalition army and gave the French a magnificent victory.[59]

The Habsburgs were humiliated. The Treaty of Pressburg, signed on December 26th, 1805, shortly after the Battle of Austerlitz, formalized

[58] PBS.org. (2023, February 10). The Ulm-Austerlitz Campaign, 1805. Retrieved from PBS.org: https://www.pbs.org/empires/napoleon/n_war/campaign/page_6.html.

[59] Mark, H. W. (2023, July 13). Battle of Austerlitz. Retrieved from World History Encyclopedia: https://www.worldhistory.org/article/2253/battle-of-austerlitz/.

both the terms of the armistice between Austria and France and Austria's shame. Austria ceded significant territories to France and its allies. This included the loss of Venetia (Venice and its territories), Tyrol, and other regions in northern Italy. Other Austrian lands were distributed among the French allies. The Holy Roman Empire, which the Habsburgs had governed for hundreds of years, was formally dissolved on August 6th, 1806, when Francis abdicated the throne.

Because of the defeat at Austerlitz, Austria underwent a period of military reorganization and reform. This period of reform aimed to address some of the shortcomings exposed at Austerlitz and prepare Austria for future conflicts. In the meantime, Austria was a defeated nation, and its military was discredited.

Diplomatic Maneuvers

Frustrated on the battlefield, the Habsburg rulers of Austria considered diplomacy to checkmate Napoleon. It would be challenging to find another skilled diplomat like Kaunitz, but Austria was fortunate to find an equally adept man at handling international negotiations.

Klemens von Metternich was skilled in diplomacy and rose through the ranks until he was made foreign minister of the Austrian Empire in 1809. He understood it would take more than cannons and bullets to defeat Napoleon. Subtle and effective diplomacy, combined with some luck, might achieve the goal.

Metternich faced many significant challenges from 1809 to 1814, the later stages of the Napoleonic Wars. These challenges tested his diplomatic skills and statesmanship as he navigated the complex and ever-shifting European political landscape. Maintaining a delicate balance in Austria's relations with Napoleon Bonaparte was a constant test. Metternich had to engage in diplomacy with the French emperor while safeguarding Austrian interests.

As Metternich decided what to do on the diplomatic front, events were unfolding that had terrible results for the Austrian Empire. The Fifth Coalition against Napoleon was formed. The War of the Fifth Coalition pitted Austria and its allies against the French. (There was a Fourth Coalition (1806–1807), but Austria did not participate.) Napoleon's victories at Aspern-Essling and Wagram forced the Austrians to sue for peace and endure another humiliation.

The Treaty of Schönbrunn, signed on October 14th, 1809, forced Austria to give up even more land, including access to the Adriatic Sea.

Austria was required to become part of Napoleon's Continental System and reduce its army to 150,000 men. A contemporary British magazine best summarized the impact of the treaty on Austria:

"This Treaty is certainly one of the most singular documents in the annals of diplomacy. We see a Christian King, calling himself the father of his people, disposing of 400,000 of his subjects, like swine in a market. We see a great and powerful Prince condescending to treat with his adversary for the brushwood of his own forests. We see the hereditary claimant of the Imperial Sceptre of Germany not only condescending to the past innovations on his own dominions, but assenting to any future alterations which the caprice or tyranny of his enemy may dictate with respect to his allies in Spain and Portugal, or to his neighbours in Italy. We see through the whole of this instrument the humiliation of the weak and unfortunate Francis, who has preferred the resignation of his fairest territories to restoring to his vassals their liberties, and giving them that interest in the public cause which their valour would have known how to protect."[60]

The Habsburgs had failed miserably on the battlefield. They next decided to use a strategy they had successfully used in the past: marriage.

Marie Louise and Napoleon

Napoleon divorced his wife Josephine on December 15th, 1809, for failing to produce a male heir. This dissolution created an irresistible opportunity that Metternich wanted to exploit. There was competition from Russia, though, as Napoleon had expressed a wish to marry Tsar Alexander I's sister. Despite that, Metternich used his diplomatic skills and flattery to convince Napoleon that the Austrian candidate, Archduchess Marie Louise, the daughter of Emperor Francis, was the best choice. The French emperor finally agreed, and the two were formally married on April 1st, 1810.

---

[60] Robertson, Angus. *The Crossroads of Civilization: A History of Vienna.* 2022.

Marriage of Napoleon I and Marie Louise.
https://commons.wikimedia.org/wiki/File:Napoleon_Marie_Louise_Marriage1.jpeg

Metternich scored a major coup with the marriage. Firstly, it established a familial connection between the Austrian and French imperial houses, potentially providing a degree of influence and leverage in future negotiations with Napoleon. The marriage alliance also brought a temporary respite to the ongoing conflict between Austria and France. It allowed Austria to secure a period of relative stability and avoid further military confrontations with Napoleon. Austria desperately needed time to regroup, and Metternich was able to guarantee that.

Napoleon's Mistakes

The French were the dominant military power in Europe, and defeating Napoleon on the battlefield was nearly impossible. It appeared only the French emperor could defeat himself. And that is precisely what happened.

Napoleon made two major blunders that would destabilize his control over Europe. The first was his invasion of Spain in 1808. Napoleon overthrew the Bourbon monarchy, putting his brother Joseph on the Spanish throne. A guerilla war on the Iberian Peninsula broke out that tied up thousands of French soldiers who were needed elsewhere. The second error in judgment was the invasion of Russia in 1812.

Napoleon's Grande Armée was destroyed in the winter snow of Russia; only a tiny fraction of the soldiers made it back alive. The Russian debacle made Napoleon vulnerable. The Sixth Coalition was thus formed.

The War of the Sixth Coalition

The primary members of the Sixth Coalition were Austria, Prussia, Russia, Great Britain, Spain, Sweden, Portugal, and Sardinia. Its goal was to overthrow Napoleon. Metternich initially tried to mediate peace, but his proposal included dismantling the Confederation of the Rhine, which Napoleon refused to do. Formal declarations of war from the coalition members followed, and Austria declared war on France in August 1813.

The most significant battle of the War of the Sixth Coalition was the Battle of Leipzig, also known as the Battle of the Nations, fought from October 16th to October 19th, 1813. It was a massive confrontation involving hundreds of thousands of troops from both sides. It was a decisive coalition victory over Napoleon's forces and marked the war's turning point, as the defeat forced Napoleon to retreat from Germany.

Metternich tried one last time to broker a peace. The Frankfurt proposals were presented to Napoleon in November. The terms called for France to return to its borders as they existed before Napoleon's expansions, permitting France to keep Belgium, Savoy, and the Rhineland. Napoleon would have to withdraw French forces from various conquered territories in Europe.

Napoleon initially showed some interest in the Frankfurt proposals, as he recognized that his position had weakened considerably after the defeat at Leipzig. However, he sought to negotiate from a place of strength and attempted to buy time for his military efforts. Ultimately, the negotiations did not lead to a peace agreement.[61]

The coalition finally invaded France and forced Napoleon to fall back to Paris. Napoleon was forced to abdicate, which he did on April 11th, 1814. The French threat was now gone, and the European powers would

---

[61] Mark, H. W. (2023, September 4). War of the Sixth Coalition. Retrieved from World History Encyclopedia: https://www.worldhistory.org/War_of_the_Sixth_Coalition/.

meet to redraw the continent's borders. The meeting, known as the Congress of Vienna, would be Metternich's finest hour.

The New Europe

The Congress of Vienna took place in Vienna, Austria, from September 1814 to June 1815. It aimed to reorganize Europe and establish a new balance of power in the continent. Representatives from Austria, Prussia, Russia, Spain, Great Britain, Portugal, Sweden, and France were in attendance.

A vital goal of the Congress of Vienna was to restore legitimate monarchs to their thrones. This would include the restoration of the Bourbon monarchy in France with Louis XVIII as king.

The Congress of Vienna intended to create a framework for stability and peaceful diplomacy in Europe. Its members understood a need for pragmatic solutions to prevent future conflicts.

The Congress of Vienna established the Concert of Europe, a series of international congresses and diplomatic meetings to resolve conflicts and maintain the balance of power in Europe. This system played a role in European diplomacy for several decades.

Significant territorial adjustments were made in Europe. Borders were redrawn, and some states gained or lost territories. Notable examples include the expansion of Prussia and the formation of the Kingdom of the Netherlands, which included the former Austrian Netherlands (Belgium).

Metternich's primary objective was to safeguard Austrian interests and restore the Habsburg monarchy to a position of prominence in Europe. He sought to regain territories lost during the Napoleonic Wars, particularly in Italy and central Europe. He advocated for establishing a balance of power in Europe to prevent any single state from becoming too dominant. This approach was instrumental in shaping the post-Napoleonic order.

Europe after the Congress of Vienna.

Alexander Altenhof, CC BY-SA 4.0 <https://creativecommons.org/licenses/by-sa/4.0>, via Wikimedia Commons; https://commons.wikimedia.org/wiki/File:Europe_1815_map_en.png

His negotiating skills enabled him to mediate disputes and engineer compromises successfully. Metternich would be a dominant figure in European politics for decades to come.[62]

<u>Age of Metternich</u>

The Age of Metternich represents a significant phase in European history that unfolded during the early to mid-19th century. It was a time of political upheaval and social change, marked by the aftermath of the Napoleonic Wars and the rise of nationalist and revolutionary movements.

Metternich's influence on European diplomacy and the balance of power was profound. His primary goals during this era were centered around maintaining conservative monarchies, containing revolutionary forces, and preserving the equilibrium of power among European nations.

Following the upheaval of the French Revolution and the Napoleonic Wars, many European monarchies had been threatened or overthrown. Metternich, representing the interests of the Austrian Empire and other

---

[62] History Guild. (2023, November 11). The Congress of Vienna. Retrieved from Historyguid.org: https://historyguild.org/the-congress-of-vienna/.

conservative states, sought to restore and maintain these traditional monarchies. He believed that solid and legitimate monarchies were essential for stability and the preservation of the social hierarchy. Consequently, many exiled monarchs were restored to their thrones, and the influence of revolutionary movements was curtailed in many parts of Europe.

An essential means of maintaining stability during this period was the Concert of Europe. Major European powers cooperated diplomatically to address common issues and contributed to preserving the balance of power. This framework facilitated discussions and negotiations, reducing the likelihood of significant conflicts. One negative result was that the more conservative members used the Concert of Europe to restrict liberal movements.

While it cannot be denied that this era suppressed liberal and nationalist aspirations, it also brought relative stability to a continent that had been in turmoil for years. Klemens von Metternich's diplomatic efforts and policies left a lasting mark on European politics and paved the way for a more peaceful, albeit complex, era in European history.

Under Metternich's influence, the Austrian Empire became a bastion of European conservatism. Austria was a key player in the Holy Alliance, which sought to maintain the conservative order in Europe. The Holy Alliance was a coalition of European monarchies formed after the Napoleonic Wars to promote conservative principles, suppress revolutionary movements, and maintain peace. While it did help to maintain the status quo, the day finally came when the Holy Alliance could no longer hold back the tide of liberalism. Habsburg Austria was caught up in the current.

Chapter 11: The Dual Monarchy

The Dual Monarchy, known as Kiegyezés in Hungarian, was a pivotal moment in the history of the Habsburg Empire. The Austro-Hungarian Compromise of 1867 created a dual monarchy, transforming the Austrian Empire into the Austro-Hungarian Empire. The compromise was a response to growing nationalist sentiments within the Austrian Empire and sought to balance the aspirations of the Austrian and Hungarian populations while maintaining Habsburg rule.

Revolution in the Air

To understand the Austro-Hungarian Compromise of 1867, one must first grasp the turbulent history of the Habsburg Empire in the 19th century. The empire was a vast, multi-ethnic state that included numerous nationalities, languages, and cultures. The Habsburg rulers faced the challenge of governing these diverse territories while preserving the power and unity of the empire.

Klemens von Metternich wanted to create stability in a Europe that had been devastated by the Napoleonic Wars. His model of governance had a reactionary design because he believed that the status quo ensured peace and quiet. The Austrian statesman hoped to create a lasting era of peace, but he would be disappointed.

The French Revolution and the Napoleonic era unleashed a yearning for greater personal freedom and the end of authoritative monarchies. Despite the Congress of Vienna and the harsh repression of European monarchies, the desire for liberty, equality, and fraternity was in the air. The French Revolution had let the genie out of the bottle, and it refused to go back in.

The Status of the Austrian Empire

The Austrian Empire, which was under the rule of the Habsburg dynasty in the early 19th century, was a multi-ethnic conglomerate consisting of various nationalities, including Germans, Hungarians, Czechs, Poles, Italians, and many others. This diversity created a complex political and social landscape, with different ethnic groups often asserting their distinct identities and demands.

Emperor Francis I and his successor presided over an absolutist monarchy characterized by centralized control and limited political representation. Dissatisfaction with the conservative and autocratic regime simmered among various segments of the population, setting the stage for revolutionary movements.

The Habsburgs did enact some reforms in the 1830s. However, these reforms were insufficient to address the deep-seated issues of national identity and political representation. The Habsburg monarchy remained the absolute power, and discontent continued to simmer beneath the surface.

Yet, the Austrian Empire also experienced economic growth and prosperity. The population of the empire increased, and the significant budget deficits caused by the Napoleonic Wars were nearly erased.

1848, Annus Revolutionis

A local uprising in January 1848 in Sicily spread like a forest fire to France, Germany, Italy, and Austria. These revolts sought to challenge established monarchies. Uprisings occurred throughout the Austrian Empire. Groups wanted to achieve either independence or greater autonomy. On March 13th, 1848, Metternich was forced to resign. A series of liberal governments followed, but the political situation continued to get out of control.

Austria's forces had to confront a volatile situation in northern Italy, and there was also unrest in Bohemia. The insurgents in northern Italy were defeated by Field Marshal Joseph Radetzky in 1849, and a period of repression in Lombardy-Venetia sponsored by the Austrians was severe. The trouble in Prague was put down, but Austria faced a more significant problem that, if unresolved, would tear the empire to pieces.

The Hungarian Question

Hungary was a diverse and multi-ethnic region within the Austrian Empire, encompassing not only ethnic Hungarians but also various minority groups, including Slovaks, Croats, Serbs, and Romanians. This ethnic diversity added complexity to Hungary's quest for autonomy and self-determination. The Hungarian Diet wielded significant power within the kingdom, and Hungary enjoyed a degree of independence in domestic affairs.

There had been some economic hardships in Hungary, which sparked discontent. A larger instigator of unrest was the spread of liberal ideas in a land where aristocrats ruled. On March 15th, 1848, Hungarian intellectuals, including Lajos Kossuth, met in Pest and drafted a revolutionary document called the Twelve Points.

The brainchild of Sándor Petőfi, the Twelve Points were a call for individual liberties and a practical blueprint for a nation. Petőfi insisted on freedom of the press and no more censorship. He also demanded the end of separate laws for the nobility and equality under the law. Religious liberty should be granted; the days of state-sponsored religion would be over. The final vestiges of the feudal system, particularly serfdom, were to be done away with.

The ideas for a nation-state were dramatic. The Twelve Points insisted that Hungary be a nation and not a part of the Austrian Empire. A national bank and a separate currency would be instituted along with an independent government with a national assembly of members whom the people elected, not the aristocracy.

The demands were presented to a weakened Austrian government, which initially accepted the demands on April 11th, 1848. Lajos Kossuth emerged as a charismatic leader of the Hungarian Revolution. His impassioned speeches and emotional commitment to Hungarian independence galvanized support for the cause. Ultimately, Kossuth declared an independent Kingdom of Hungary.[63]

---

[63] Sellers, W. (2023, March 13). Opinion: The Forgotten Hungarian Revolution. Retrieved from Alabama Political Reporter: https://www.alreporter.com/2023/03/13/opinion-the-forgotten-hungarian-revolution/.

Kossuth inspiring followers in a speech he gave in 1848.
https://commons.wikimedia.org/wiki/File:Kollarz_Kossuth_Cegl%C3%A9den_1848.JPG

A significant problem with all of this was the way the Hungarians treated ethnic minorities. There were many ethnic groups in Hungary, but most of their needs were largely ignored. Croats, Slovaks, Serbs, and other groups within Hungary preferred the protection of the central government in Vienna. War broke out in the autumn of 1848 as Hungarians fought the Austrians and Croats.

Austria finally appealed to Russia for help. Russian troops assisted in ending the armed conflict in Hungary. The Hungarian attempt at liberty was officially over, but there were still issues that desperately needed to be addressed. The Austrian Empire could not exist in its current form, and its many minorities would continue to insist on some degree of independence. Vienna knew there had to be a resolution to the problems that surfaced in 1848.[64]

Franz Joseph, The Last Best Hope of the Habsburgs

Russian regiments restored calm in the Austrian Empire, but they could not restore the status quo. The past imperial authority had been

---

[64] Heritage History. (2023, October 30). Hungarian Revolution. Retrieved from Heritage-History.com: https://www.heritage-history.com/index.php?c=resources&s=war-dir&f=wars_hungarian.

violently compromised. Hungary was another war waiting to happen, and other ethnic minorities were demanding concessions. The Habsburgs had to come up with a workable answer to the problems the 1848 unrest brought out of the shadows.

In the past, the Habsburgs were able to produce a monarch at critical times to meet impossible challenges. This happened in 1848 when Franz Joseph became the Austrian emperor. He was eighteen years old, but he quickly showed he had the maturity of someone twenty years older. Franz Joseph understood the gravity of the situation and the potential threat posed by the revolutionary movements.

He initially sought to maintain the traditional absolute monarchy and resist the demands for constitutional reforms and national self-determination. He was proclaimed emperor on December 2nd, 1848, after the former emperor, Ferdinand, abdicated. That abdication was the final act in a year in which the old order had been purged. Metternich had resigned, and Emperor Ferdinand approved a Hungarian constitution, which kept the emperor as monarch; that constitution was suspended in 1849. The arrival of Russian troops ended the crisis in Hungary. Unfortunately, Franz Joseph had a new set of problems to the south in Italy.

Franz Joseph in 1892.
https://commons.wikimedia.org/wiki/File:Emperor_Francis_Joseph.jpg

Creation of the Italian State

The 1848 revolutionary wave that swept across Europe reached the Italian states, and many Italians sought to overthrow their rulers and establish independent, unified nation-states. The Lombardy-Venetia region was a particular hotspot for revolutionary activity.

The First Italian War of Independence started in 1848 with rebellions in Milan and Venice. On March 23rd, 1848, the Kingdom of Sardinia-Piedmont, led by King Charles Albert, declared war on Austria, intending to liberate northern Italy from Habsburg rule. Franz Joseph was able to win this contest, but one of the Italian leaders, Giuseppe Garibaldi, would give the Austrians headaches in the future.

Italy was caught up in a revolutionary spirit known as irredentism, which called for the liberation of Italians living under foreign rule and their incorporation into a unified Italian state. This meant the Habsburg possessions in Italy would be targeted.

Austria also faced France in the Second War of Italian Independence. Fighting against the French was a hopeless situation, and the Battle of Solferino on June 24th, 1859, saw Austria give Lombardy to France, which, in turn, transferred the territory to Sardinia.

Meanwhile, the situation in Hungary was still simmering in the background.

An Untenable Situation

Austria had Hungary under tight military control after the Hungarian Revolution of 1848, but the people in Hungary had not calmed down. The status quo was no longer something that could be maintained. Either some agreement had to be reached, or Austria would be continually fighting to keep control over Hungary. The latter was an expensive option, and Austria could not afford the cost.[65]

The threat of non-stop warfare was not the only motivation behind a permanent solution. Emperor Franz Joseph wanted to maintain the unity and stability of the Austrian Empire. He recognized that the empire faced significant challenges, including the rise of Hungarian nationalism. By agreeing to a compromise, he aimed to secure Hungary's loyalty and cooperation, which would contribute to the empire's stability.

---

[65] DBpedia.org. (2023, October 30). Austro-Hungarian Compromise of 1867. Retrieved from DBpedia.org: https://dbpedia.org/page/Austro-Hungarian_Compromise_of_1867.

Economic considerations also played a role. Hungary, with its fertile lands and agricultural resources, sought control over economic policies that would benefit its own economy. This was particularly important given Hungary's rustic nature.

The Negotiators

Emperor Franz Joseph relied on Friedrich Ferdinand von Beust to navigate the complexities of the negotiations. Von Beust was motivated by the emperor's objectives, seeking a compromise that would satisfy Hungarian demands while preserving the Habsburg monarchy's influence in foreign affairs and defense.

The principal Hungarian negotiators were Ferenc Deák and Count Gyula Andrássy. Deák is often referred to as the "Sage of the Country" and was a prominent Hungarian statesman. His primary motive was to secure greater political and economic autonomy for Hungary. He was a moderate nationalist who believed that cooperation with the Habsburg monarchy was more beneficial than outright separatism.

Andrássy advocated for a compromise that would grant Hungary substantial autonomy. His motives were aligned with Deák's in seeking a peaceful resolution to the Hungarian question. He believed securing Hungary's rights and privileges through negotiation was preferable to risking armed conflict.

What is significant about the negotiations is that there were no strong adversaries at the table. Both sides wanted to avoid war, and everyone was looking for an agreeable way in which Austria and Hungary could still maintain a relationship while giving the latter greater autonomy than before.

The Ausgleich

The year 1866 was a terrible one for Austria. It was involved in the Third Italian War of Independence and fought against the Kingdom of Italy, which was supported by Prussia. Furthermore, Austria was fighting Prussia in the Austro-Prussian War. By the time the shooting stopped, Austria had ceded Venetia to France, which then handed it over to Italy. This marked another significant loss of Italian territories under Franz Joseph's rule. The next year, 1867, would be much better for Austria and the Habsburgs.

The Austro-Hungarian Compromise of 1867, also known as the Ausgleich, was a pivotal event in the history of the Habsburg monarchy. This compromise established the dual monarchy of Austria-Hungary, transforming the political structure of the Austrian Empire. The Austria-Hungary Compromise of 1867 consisted of several key points.

- Establishment of the Dual Monarchy: The Austro-Hungarian Compromise recognized Austria and Hungary as two separate yet equal states within a shared monarchy. Emperor Franz Joseph I remained the common head of state, serving as the emperor of Austria and the king of Hungary.
- Hungarian autonomy: Hungary was granted considerable autonomy in domestic affairs. It had its own parliament (the Diet), government, and legal system, allowing Hungarians to legislate and administer their internal affairs independently.
- Shared institutions: While domestic affairs were largely the purview of each state, certain areas were managed jointly, like foreign policy, defense, and finance. Shared ministerial councils, known as common ministry councils, were established to oversee these shared matters.
- Language rights: The Austro-Hungarian Compromise recognized the Hungarian language alongside German as an official language of the empire, signifying the linguistic diversity within Austria-Hungary.

A compromise only happens when both sides concede points to arrive at a consensus. Austria acknowledged Hungary's autonomy in domestic affairs, allowing the Hungarian Diet to legislate and govern independently. Austria also recognized the restoration of Hungary's historic constitution and the Hungarian legal system. Hungary recognized the Habsburg monarchy and Emperor Franz Joseph I as the common ruler. Hungarian leaders agreed to participate in the common ministries responsible for foreign affairs, defense, and finance, in which they had a say but did not hold absolute control.[66]

The Austro-Hungarian Compromise of 1867 had significant long-term consequences:

- Stability: In the short term, the compromise provided a degree of peace to the Habsburg monarchy by addressing the Hungarian question and providing a framework for governance.

[66] Study.com. (2023, October 30). The Dual Monarchy of Austria-Hungary. Retrieved from Study.com: https://study.com/learn/lesson/hungarian-austrian-dual-monarchy-ausgleich.html#:~:text=The%20Ausgleich%2C%20or%20the%20formal,Ferenc%20Deak%2C%20and%20other%20delegates.

- Nationalism and ethnic tensions: While the compromise successfully quelled immediate nationalist demands, it did not fully address the underlying ethnic and national tensions within the empire. The multinational character of Austria-Hungary continued to be a source of conflict and discontent.

Unfortunately, the compromise created an asymmetrical structure, with Hungary having more autonomy and influence in domestic affairs than Austria. This imbalance fueled resentment and tensions within the empire.

The Austro-Hungarian Compromise's legacy is marked by the precarious coexistence of diverse ethnic groups and the eventual dissolution of Austria-Hungary in the aftermath of World War I, which marked the end of the Habsburg monarchy.

Chapter 12: The End of the Habsburg Dynasty

The Austro-Prussian War was short, and it heralded the end of an era in central European history. Austria was no longer the premier German state; the new Kingdom of Germany had replaced it. The Habsburg Empire was now Austria-Hungary. It was still an enormous state in Europe, but Great Britain, France, and Germany now contested for pride of place. The Habsburgs' power was eclipsed, but that did not mean their empire was a backwater. Austria-Hungary would play a significant role in the cultural and intellectual life of Europe in the late 19th century.

<u>The Cultural Mecca of Europe</u>

Vienna, the capital of the Habsburg Empire, emerged as a vibrant cultural hub during the late 19th and early 20th centuries. It is often referred to as the "City of Dreams." Vienna experienced a remarkable cultural renaissance in the late 19th and early 20th centuries. This period, known as the "Viennese fin de siècle ("end of the century"), was characterized by a flourishing of artistic, intellectual, and social movements that propelled the city onto the global stage. A convergence of factors, such as political stability, imperial patronage, and a rich cultural tradition, gave rise to Vienna's prominence as a cultural hub.

At the end of the 19th century, Vienna was the destination for many of the empire's subjects. Italians, Slovaks, Poles, Slovenians, Moravians, Germans, and Slovaks immigrated to the capital city, attracted by its many opportunities. In 1910, Vienna had a population of two million and was a liberal and cosmopolitan center. The Viennese melting pot welcomed universal forms of communication and artistic expression.[67]

The Arts

The Vienna Secession was a groundbreaking art movement that emerged in 1897 as a reaction against academic conservatism. It was the formal beginning of modern art in a country with a conservative tradition. Led by a group of avant-garde artists, including Gustav Klimt, Koloman Moser, and Josef Hoffmann, the Secessionists sought to break free from traditional artistic norms. Their motto, "To each age its art, and to art its freedom," encapsulated their desire for creative autonomy. The work of this art group is the Austrian version of the Art Nouveau style of painting.

The Vienna Secession was known for intricate symbolism, sensuality, and decorative patterns. The Secessionists built the first permanent exhibition space dedicated to displaying contemporary art, which still exists.[68]

The Kiss by Gustav Klimt.
https://en.wikipedia.org/wiki/File:The_Kiss_-_Gustav_Klimt_-_Google_Cultural_Institute.jpg

---

[67] The Economist. (2016, December 24). How Vienna Produced Ideas That Shaped the West. Retrieved from Economist.com: https://www.economist.com/christmas-specials/2016/12/24/how-vienna-produced-ideas-that-shaped-the-west.
[68] The Art Story. (20232, October 31). Summary of the Vienna Secession. Retrieved from Theartsotry.org: https://www.theartstory.org/movement/vienna-secession/.

Die Musik

Vienna's significance in music has been undeniable throughout history, particularly during the late 19th and early 20th centuries. This period witnessed a dynamic interplay of traditionalism and innovation, exemplified by the composers who either adhered to or challenged established norms. From late Romanticism to the pioneering works of the Second Viennese School, Vienna stood at the forefront of musical exploration. It earned its title as "The City of Music."

The late 19th century in Vienna was marked by the presence of Johannes Brahms, a composer known for his mastery of classical forms and profound emotional depth. Brahms, with his four symphonies, numerous chamber works, and songs, played a pivotal role in preserving and advancing the Romantic tradition. Brahams was both a traditionalist and an innovator. He followed the basic structures of the Classical tradition but used the intense expression of the Romantic movement when creating his works.[69]

Johann Strauss II was a composer of light music that is still immensely popular. Referred to as the "Waltz King," Strauss is one of the most iconic figures in the history of Viennese music. His music and compositions are closely associated with Vienna, and he played a pivotal role in shaping the city's musical and cultural identity during the 19th century.

His melodies were known for their charm, elegance, and infectious rhythms, making them immensely popular at social events and balls. Strauss also composed operettas, light operas known for their humor and catchy tunes. His most famous operetta, *Die Fledermaus* (*The Bat*), premiered in 1874 and remains a staple of the operetta repertoire. "The Blue Danube" is known by most people today. His waltzes continue to have public appeal.

Johann Strauss II's music became synonymous with the elegance, grace, and joie de vivre of Viennese society during the 19th century. His compositions captured the spirit of the city and reflected the optimism and charm of the Habsburg era. The music he wrote was a central part of Vienna's vibrant ball culture. His compositions were featured at

---

[69] Classicfm.com. (2023, October 31). Johannes Brahms. Retrieved from Classicfm.com: https://www.classicfm.com/composers/brahms/.

countless balls, including the famous Vienna Opera Ball.[70]

There were significant venues where the music of Vienna was performed. The Vienna Philharmonic, founded in 1842, was a vital institution. It became renowned for its annual New Year's Concert, which celebrated the Strauss family's waltzes and other Viennese classics. The Vienna State Opera was a premier venue for operatic performances. During this period, it showcased works by composers of the day, including Richard Strauss and Gustav Mahler.

<u>Intellectual Discourse</u>

Vienna's cultural renaissance extended beyond the visual arts to encompass literature, philosophy, and music. The city was home to some of the most influential intellectual circles in Europe. The city's coffeehouses, such as Café Central and Café Griensteidl, served as meeting places for artists, musicians, and intellectuals. These establishments facilitated the exchange of ideas and contributed to the city's vibrant cultural scene.

The Vienna Circle originated in 1907 and began to formulate philosophical concepts of a positivist view of science. The psychoanalytic movement, which started in Vienna, produced substantial insights into psychology and the study of human behavior.

Sigmund Freud is considered the father of psychoanalysis. He developed a groundbreaking approach to understanding the human mind, which he initially called the "talking cure." Freud's theory emphasized the role of the unconscious mind and the impact of repressed thoughts, memories, and desires on an individual's behavior. His work challenged prevailing psychological and psychiatric paradigms. The concept of the "talking cure" involved free association and open dialog to explore a patient's unconscious thoughts and emotions. This approach aimed to uncover repressed traumas and conflicts, thereby providing insight and relief to individuals suffering from mental disorders.[71]

[70] Classicfm.com. (2023, October 31). Johann Strauss II: A Life. Retrieved from Classicfm.com: https://www.classicfm.com/composers/strauss-ii/guides/johann-strauss-ii-life/.
[71] Christopher Marx, C. B. (2017, September 17). Talking Cure Models: A Framework of Analysis. Retrieved from National Library of Medicine: https://www.ncbi.nlm.nih.gov/pmc/articles/PMC5601393/#:~:text=The%20%E2%80%9Ctalking%20cure%2C%E2%80%9D%20then,the%20patient%20from%20hysteric%20symptoms.

Freud's colleagues and students, including Carl Jung, Alfred Adler, and Otto Rank, played significant roles in developing psychoanalysis as a field of study and clinical practice. The psychoanalytic movement of the late 19th century was a revolutionary development in psychology and the understanding of the human mind. This movement laid the foundation for modern psychoanalysis and profoundly influenced the fields of psychology, psychiatry, and psychotherapy. It was part of the exciting time of expression and innovative thoughts that made Vienna and Habsburg Austria-Hungary shine.

The Creeping Shadows

Cabaret is a popular musical that depicts café society with all its delights and sophistication. It is juxtaposed against the fall of the Weimar Republic and the militancy of national socialism. This is nearly the same setting for late Habsburg society. Vienna's cultural vitality in the late 19th and early 20th centuries was a testament to the city's ability to foster artistic, intellectual, and musical innovation. The energy and vitality distracted people's attention from what was happening outside of the cultural circles.

Europe had not seen a major conflict since the Franco-Prussian War. There were localized wars in the Balkans, but nothing compared to the Napoleonic Wars. The happy scenes were soon to come to an end as the twilight years of the Habsburgs began.

Prelude to a War

The period from 1900 to 1914 was marked by a complex interplay of political, diplomatic, economic, and military factors in Europe that contributed to the outbreak of World War I. Austria-Hungary, under the rule of Emperor Franz Joseph, was a central player in the events that led to the war. While Franz Joseph might not have been personally seeking war, his actions and policies did not prevent the escalation of tensions.

The major European powers, including Austria-Hungary, were engaged in imperial rivalries and competition for colonial territories. This animosity created tensions between these powers, especially Germany, France, and Great Britain.

The complex system of alliances, such as the Triple Entente (France, Russia, and Great Britain) and the Triple Alliance (Germany, Austria-Hungary, and Italy), created a situation where a regional conflict could quickly escalate into a larger war. Austria-Hungary had the support of

Germany, while Serbia had the backing of Russia.

The Balkans

Balkan nationalists saw an opportunity with the decay of the Ottoman Empire to end hundreds of years of Turkish control. Several wars, beginning in 1912, saw various regions in the Balkans struggle for independence or border expansion. It was not just the Ottomans versus the Christians; Bulgaria, Serbia, and Romania were also locked in intense struggles with each other.[72]

The region was not stable, and there was an opportunity for Austria-Hungary to make territorial gains. This was risky because fervent nationalism was driving emotions to agitated states. Despite the potential hazards, Austria-Hungary annexed Bosnia and Herzegovina in 1908, which angered Serbia.

The major alliances had interests in the Balkans. Russia had a historical and cultural connection to the Slavic peoples of the Balkans, particularly in Serbia. France had historical alliances with Russia, and Great Britain was concerned about maintaining the balance of power in Europe.

The Major Alliances Drift toward War

Barbara Tuchman's book *The Guns of August* provides a detailed analysis of the relationships between the Triple Entente and the Triple Alliance in the years leading up to the outbreak of World War I. The leaders within both alliances made assumptions about their adversaries' intentions, which played a role in the escalation of tensions.

A naval arms race already existed between Germany and Great Britain. Germany's expansion of its High Seas Fleet and Great Britain's response with the construction of new battleships added to the overall sense of insecurity. Detailed war plans, such as the Schlieffen Plan in Germany, were created with the assumption of an impending conflict. These plans involved complex timetables and troop movements that required meticulous execution.

Military posturing was rapidly replacing pragmatic diplomacy in resolving differences. A fundamental assumption was that alliances were a deterrent to war. The possibility of a chain reaction, including mobilizations and counter-mobilizations, was viewed as making the

---

[72] Hall, R. C. (2018, April 4). War in the Balkans. Retrieved from International Encyclopedia of the First World War: https://encyclopedia.1914-1918-online.net/article/war_in_the_balkans.

outbreak of a major war unlikely. Only a madman would start the martial ball rolling. Perhaps all it would take was a passionate nationalist.

The Shot Heard 'Round the World

Gavrilo Princip was a teenage member of the Young Bosnia movement. Learning that the heir to the throne of Austria-Hungary, Archduke Ferdinand, and his wife were paying a visit to Sarajevo, Bosnia, Princip and his comrades hatched a plan to assassinate the archduke. The conspirators made their way to Sarajevo. On June 28th, 1914, after multiple attempts by the assassins, Princip fired his pistol at point-blank range and killed the couple.

Austria-Hungary blamed Serbia for the assassination and issued an ultimatum on July 23rd, 1914 (the July Ultimatum) that, if not met, would result in war. Russia made it clear that it would support Serbia. Austria-Hungary sought assurances from Germany of support, which were granted. One month after the death of Archduke Ferdinand, on July 28th, Austria-Hungary declared war on Serbia. Germany, France, Russia, and Great Britain then issued declarations of war. World War I began.[73]

Emperor Franz Joseph of Austria-Hungary was not the principal instigator of the conflict, but his leadership and decisions as the monarch of Austria-Hungary were instrumental in the chain of events that led to the outbreak of war. Rather than actively pursue diplomatic solutions to the crisis, Franz Joseph and his government opted for a path of military action against Serbia.

Austria-Hungary in World War I

Austria-Hungary played a significant role in World War I as one of the Central Powers (Germany, Austria-Hungary, Bulgaria, and the Ottoman Empire). The empire faced numerous challenges on various fronts. Austria-Hungary was heavily involved in the Eastern Front of the war, where it faced off against Russia. The eastern theater of the war saw significant fighting, and Austria-Hungary struggled with the vast expanse of the front and the pressure exerted by the Russian army.

Austria-Hungary also dealt with the Italians. Italy, which was initially a member of the Triple Alliance but later switched sides to join the Triple Entente, declared war on Austria-Hungary on May 23rd, 1915. The two countries confronted each other in an Alpine war that mirrored the

---

[73] History. (2021, June 25). Austria's Archduke Ferdinand Assassinated. Retrieved from History.com: https://www.history.com/this-day-in-history/archduke-ferdinand-assassinated.

Western Front in its stalemates.

Austria-Hungary faced significant military challenges during the war. Its forces struggled on multiple fronts, and the empire's military and logistical capabilities were stretched thin. The Dual Monarchy often relied on German support, particularly from 1917 onward.

The war imposed a heavy economic and social burden on Austria-Hungary. The empire faced shortages of food and supplies, which led to discontent and unrest among the civilian population.

Emperor Franz Joseph, who had ruled for over six decades, died on November 21st, 1916. He was succeeded by his grandnephew, Charles I, who attempted to seek a separate peace with the Triple Entente. However, these efforts were unsuccessful, and Austria-Hungary remained committed to its alliance with Germany.

By 1918, Austria-Hungary was in a state of disarray. Its armies were on the retreat on multiple fronts, and the internal cohesion of the empire was eroding due to ethnic tensions and nationalist movements. It was increasingly clear that Austria-Hungary was going to lose the war. Strikes and street demonstrations served to drive the final nail into the coffin. On October 17th, 1918, the Hungarian Parliament declared Hungary's independence, effectively dissolving the Austro-Hungarian Empire.

The Final Dissolution

With the dissolution of the empire and the signing of the Armistice of Villa Giusti with Italy on November 3rd, 1918, Austria-Hungary effectively withdrew from World War I. Charles I went into exile, and the empire disintegrated into several successor states.

The end of the empire became official with the Treaty of Saint-Germain-en-Laye on September 10th, 1919, and the Treaty of Trianon on June 4th, 1920. Austria lost 60 percent of its old territory, and Hungary lost 72 percent of its former territory. The land was divided among several existing nations, and new states were created. Austria passed the Habsburg Law on April 3rd, 1919, which dethroned the Habsburgs and banished them from all Austrian territory.

Austria's association with the Habsburg dynasty, which had existed for hundreds of years, was over. All that was left of the Habsburgs were the magnificent palaces, the stunning art collections, and the beautiful music. All their political power was gone.

The dissolution of Austria-Hungary after WWI.
Österreich-Ungarns_Ende.png: AlphaCentauri / derivative work: P. S. Burton, CC BY-SA 3.0
<http://creativecommons.org/licenses/by-sa/3.0/>, via Wikimedia Commons;
https://commons.wikimedia.org/wiki/File:Dissolution_of_Austria-Hungary.png

Conclusion

The Habsburg dynasty lasted longer than many ruling families. Hundreds of years of Habsburg rule in central Europe created countries and instituted policies that impacted the modern era. The influence the Habsburgs had on the culture and the politics of Europe and beyond is significant.

Although the Habsburgs did engage in war, their greatest success came with diplomacy. They used marriages and treaties to gain more with less bloodshed. It reminds us that negotiations can be more effective than guns and bullets.

The cultural gifts that the Habsburgs left were tremendous. We can still view the artwork and the architecture the Habsburgs commissioned. It is thanks in part to the Habsburgs that astronomy progressed beyond the opinion of Aristotle and is based more on science and mathematics than Christianity. We are the beneficiaries of the patronage that the Habsburgs generously provided.

Unfortunately for the Habsburgs, diplomacy finally failed them in the early years of the 20th century. The Habsburgs fell victim to nationalism and extreme policies that made war the only way to resolve issues.

The Habsburgs were a unique ruling family in Europe's history. They added more to Western civilization than they ever took from it. Anyone who has seen the Schönbrunn Palace in Vienna or El Escorial in Spain will know that. The family legacy provided new standards for culture and the arts, and they were an amazing line of monarchs. They were prominent contributors to Western civilization.

If you enjoyed this book, a review on Amazon would be greatly appreciated because it would mean a lot to hear from you.

To leave a review:

1. Open your camera app.
2. Point your mobile device at the **QR** code.
3. The review page will appear in your web browser.

Thanks for your support!

Here's another book by Enthralling History that you might like

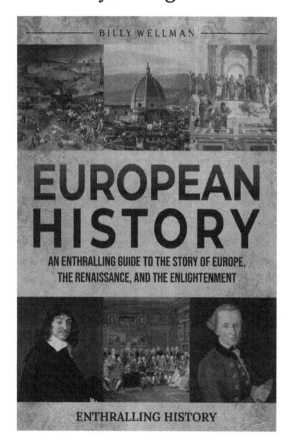

Free limited time bonus

Stop for a moment. We have a free bonus set up for you. The problem is this: we forget 90% of everything that we read after 7 days. Crazy fact, right? Here's the solution: we've created a printable, 1-page pdf summary for this book that you're reading now. All you have to do to get your free pdf summary is to go to the following website: **https://livetolearn.lpages.co/enthrallinghistory/**

Or, Scan the QR code!

Once you do, it will be intuitive. Enjoy, and thank you!

Bibliography

History's Women. (2023, November 8). Maria Theresa. Retrieved from History's Women: https://historyswomen.com/women-who-ruled/maria-theresa/.

Abernethy, S. (2013, May 3). Charles the Bold, Duke of Burgundy. Retrieved from The Freelance History Writer: https://thefreelancehistorywriter.com/2013/05/03/charles-the-bold-duke-of-burgundy/.

Biography.com. (2021, October 21). Maria Theresa. Retrieved from Biography.com: https://www.biography.com/royalty/maria-theresa.

Britannica.com. (2023, November 8). Conflicts with Revolutionary France, 1790-1805. Retrieved from Britannica.com: https://www.britannica.com/place/Austria/Conflicts-with-revolutionary-France-1790-1805.

Britannica.com. (2023, October 26). Mature Career of Tycho Brahe. Retrieved from Britannica.com: https://www.britannica.com/biography/Tycho-Brahe-Danish-astronomer/Mature-career.

Britannica.com. (2023, October 17). Partitions of Poland. Retrieved from Britannica.com: https://www.britannica.com/event/Partitions-of-Poland.

Britannica.com. (2023, October 28). War of the Spanish Succession. Retrieved from Britannica.com: https://www.britannica.com/event/War-of-the-Spanish-Succession.

BritishBattles.com. (2023, October 28). Battle of Blenheim. Retrieved from Britishbattles.com: https://www.britishbattles.com/war-of-the-spanish-succession/battle-of-blenheim/.

Canun, N. (2022, March 21). 5 Most Brutal Conquistadors of the New World. Retrieved from Spanish Academy: https://www.spanish.academy/blog/5-most-brutal-conquistadors-of-the-new-world/.

Cavendish, R. (2007, November). Spanish Bankruptcy. Retrieved from History Today: https://www.historytoday.com/archive/spanish-bankruptcy.

Christopher Marx, C. B. (2017, September 17). Talking Cure Models: A Framework of Analysis. Retrieved from National Library of Medicine: https://www.ncbi.nlm.nih.gov/pmc/articles/PMC5601393/#:~:text=The%20%E2%80%9Ctalking%20cure%2C%E2%80%9D%20then,the%20patient%20from%20hysteric%20symptoms.

Classicfm.com. (2023, October 31). Johann Strauss II: A Life. Retrieved from Classicfm.com: https://www.classicfm.com/composers/strauss-ii/guides/johann-strauss-ii-life/.

Classicfm.com. (2023, October 31). Johannes Brahms. Retrieved from Classicfm.com: https://www.classicfm.com/composers/brahms/.

DailyHistory.org. (2023, October 28). How Did the Peace of Augsburg (1555) Lead to the Thirty Years' War (1618-1648). Retrieved from DailyHistory.org: https://dailyhistory.org/How_did_the_Peace_of_Augsburg_(1555)_lead_to_the_Thirty

 Years War (1618-1648).

DBpedia.org. (2023, October 30). Austro-Hungarian Compromise of 1867. Retrieved from DBpedia.org: https://dbpedia.org/page/Austro-Hungarian_Compromise_of_1867.

Encyclopedia.com. (2023, October 25). Mining, The Americas. Retrieved from Encyclopedia.com: https://www.encyclopedia.com/history/encyclopedias-almanacs-transcripts-and-maps/mining-americas.

Famous Scientists. (2023, October 26). Johannes Kepler. Retrieved from Famousscientists.org: https://www.famousscientists.org/johannes-kepler/.

Ferdinand, M. d. (2023, September 17). Charles V Holy Roman Emperor. Retrieved from Britannica.com: https://www.britannica.com/biography/Charles-V-Holy-Roman-emperor.

Flantzer, S. (2023, May 29). Mary, Duchess of Burgundy, Archduchess of Austria. Retrieved from Unofficial Royalty: https://www.unofficialroyalty.com/mary-duchess-of-burgundy-archduchess-of-austria/.

Friehs, J. T. (2023, October 25). Working at Court I: Pro and Contra. Retrieved from The World of the Habsburgs: https://www.habsburger.net/en/chapter/working-court-i-pro-and-contra.

Getlen, L. (2015, July 26). Meet the World's Richest Man Who Changed Christianity. Retrieved from New York Post.com:

https://nypost.com/2015/07/26/meet-historys-richest-man-who-changed-christianity/.

Gruber, S. (2023, November 8). Maria Theresa: The "Great Reformer." Retrieved from The World of the Habsburgs: https://www.habsburger.net/en/chapter/maria-theresa-great-reformer.

Gruber, S. (2023, October 28). Wallenstein: Death by Murder. Retrieved from The World of the Habsburgs: https://www.habsburger.net/en/chapter/wallenstein-death-murder.

Hall, R. C. (2018, April 4). War in the Balkans. Retrieved from International Encyclopedia of the First World War: https://encyclopedia.1914-1918-online.net/article/war_in_the_balkans.

Heath, R. (2023, October 21). Emperor Charles V and the Fugger Family. Retrieved from Emperor Charles V: https://www.emperorcharlesv.com/charles-v-fugger-family/.

Heritage History. (2023, October 30). Hungarian Revolution. Retrieved from Heritage-History.com: https://www.heritage-history.com/index.php?c=resources&s=war-dir&f=wars_hungarian.

History. (2021, June 25). Austria's Archduke Ferdinand Assassinated. Retrieved from History.com: https://www.history.com/this-day-in-history/archduke-ferdinand-assassinated.

History Guild. (2023, November 11). The Congress of Vienna. Retrieved from Historyguid.org: https://historyguild.org/the-congress-of-vienna/.

History Learning. (2023, October 28). The Edict of Restitution. Retrieved from History

Learning: https://historylearning.com/the-thirty-years-war0/edict-of-restitution/.

History Skills. (2023, September 14). The Valladolid Debate: When Europeans Argued About Whether Indigenous People Were Human. Retrieved from Historyskills.com: https://www.historyskills.com/classroom/year-8/valladolid-debate/.

Holy Roman Empire Association. (2023, October 21). Holy Roman Emperor Frederick III-1440-1493. Retrieved from Holy Roman Empire Association: http://www.holyromanempireassociation.com/holy-roman-emperor-frederick-iii-.html.

Infoplease. (2023, October 28). Thirty Years' War: The Danish Period. Retrieved from Infoplease.com: https://www.infoplease.com/encyclopedia/history/modern-europe/wars-battles/thirty-years-war/the-danish-period.

Keithly, D. M. (2008, April 3). Maria Theresa. Retrieved from Enlightenment-revolution.org: https://enlightenment-revolution.org/index.php?title=Maria_Theresa.

Kilroy-Ewbank, D. L. (2023, October 25). El Escorial, Spain. Retrieved from Khan Academy: https://www.khanacademy.org/humanities/renaissance-reformation/xa6688040:spain-portugal-15th-16th-century/xa6688040:16th-century-spain/a/el-escorial-spain.

Lumen Learning. (2023, October 28). The Peace of Westphalia and Sovereignty. Retrieved from Lumenlearning.com: https://courses.lumenlearning.com/atd-herkimer-westerncivilization/chapter/the-peace-of-westphalia-and-sovereignty/.

Lumen Learning. (2023, October 28). War of Spanish Succession. Retrieved from Lumenlearning.com: https://courses.lumenlearning.com/suny-fmcc-boundless-worldhistory/chapter/war-of-spanish-succession/.

Macgregory History. (2023, October 31). July Crisis 1914. Retrieved from Macgregoryhistory.com: https://www.macgregorishistory.com/wp-content/uploads/2020/12/WWI-July-Crisis-1914.pdf

Mark, H. W. (2023, July 13). Battle of Austerlitz. Retrieved from World History Encyclopedia: https://www.worldhistory.org/article/2253/battle-of-austerlitz/.

Mark, H. W. (2023, September 4). War of the Sixth Coalition. Retrieved from World History Encyclopedia: https://www.worldhistory.org/War_of_the_Sixth_Coalition/.

Maxwell, K. (2020, December 30). The Beginnings of Globalization: The Spanish Silver Trade Routes. Retrieved from Defense.info: https://defense.info/global-dynamics/2020/12/the-beginnings-of-globalization-the-spanish-silver-trade-routes/.

Mediakron.bc.edu. (2023, October 25). Turkish Bombard. Retrieved from Mediakron.bc.edu: https://mediakron.bc.edu/ottomans/turkish-bombard/siege-of-vienna.

Munoz, J. A. (2019, September 20). Profit vs. Usury: Difference from the Point of View of Saint Thomas Aquinas. Retrieved from The Tseconomist: https://thetseconomist.wordpress.com/2019/09/20/profit-vs-usury-difference-from-the-point-of-view-of-saint-thomas-aquinas/.

Musee Protestant. (2023, October 21). The Augsburg Confession (1530). Retrieved from Museeprotestant.org: https://museeprotestant.org/en/notice/the-augsburg-confession-1530/.

New Advent. (2023, October 28). German (Catholic) League. Retrieved from New Advent: https://www.newadvent.org/cathen/09100a.htm

New Advent. (2023, October 23). Johannes Tserclaes, County of Tilly. Retrieved from New Advent: https://www.newadvent.org/cathen/14724c.htm.

New Advent. (2023, November 8). Wenzel Anton Kaunitz. Retrieved from NewAdvent.org: https://www.newadvent.org/cathen/08611b.htm.

OAW. (2023, October 25). Music at the Courts of the House of Habsburg. Retrieved from OAW: https://www.oeaw.ac.at/acdh/projects/music-at-the-courts-of-the-house-of-habsburg.

Officeapp.live.com. (2023, October 25). Born with a Silve Spoon The Origin of World Trade in 1571. Retrieved from Officeapp.live.com: https://view.officeapps.live.com/op/view.aspx?src=https%3A%2F%2Fwww.birdvilleschools.net%2Fcms%2Flib2%2FTX01000797%2FCentricity%2FDomain%2F3775%2FBorn_with_a_Silver_SpoonThe_Origin_of_World_Trade_in_1571.doc&wdOrigin=BROWSELINK

Palffy, G. (2002). The Border Defense System in Hungary in the Sixteenth and Seventeenth Centuries. Retrieved from Academia.edu: https://www.academia.edu/539595/The_Border_Defense_System_in_Hungary_in_the_Sixteenth_and_Seventeenth_Centuries_In_A_Millennium_of_Hungarian_Military_History_Ed_L%C3%A1szl%C3%B3_Veszpr%C3%A9my_B%C3%A9la_K_Kir%C3%A1ly_New_York_Social_Science_Monographs_Bro.

Parry, V. (2023, October 25). Suleyman the Magnificent. Retrieved from Britannica.com: https://www.britannica.com/biography/Suleyman-the-Magnificent.

PBS.org. (2023, February 10). The Ulm-Austerlitz Campaign, 1805. Retrieved from PBS.org: https://www.pbs.org/empires/napoleon/n_war/campaign/page_6.html.

Radioswissclassic. (2023, October 25). Cornelius Canis. Retrieved from Radioswissclassic: https://www.radioswissclassic.ch/en/music-database/musician/54261523c37de6c3eba58ffec69f05ab13193d/biography?app=true.

Redazione. (2018, August 21). Tycho Brahe, Astronomer and Alchemist at the Court of Rudolf II. Retrieved from Progetto: http://www.progetto.cz/tycho-brahe-astronomo-e-alchimista-alla-corte-di-rodolfo-ii/?lang=en.

Robertson, Angus. The Crossroads of Civilization: A History of Vienna. 2022.

Royal Museums Greenwich. (2023, November 8). Queen Elizabeth I's Speech to the Troops at Tilbury. Retrieved from Rmg.co.uk: https://www.rmg.co.uk/stories/topics/queen-elizabeth-speech-troops-tilbury.

Schloss Schonbrunn. (2023, October 25). Architectural History: 17th and 18th Century. Retrieved from Schoenbrunn.at: https://www.schoenbrunn.at/en/about-schoenbrunn/the-palace/history/architectural-history-17th-and-early-18th-century.

Sellers, W. (2023, March 13). Opinion: The Forgotten Hungarian Revolution. Retrieved from Alabama Political Reporter:

https://www.alreporter.com/2023/03/13/opinion-the-forgotten-hungarian-revolution/.

Serlin, D. (2014, May 1). Turning the Tide: Venetian Contributions to the Battle of Lepanto. Retrieved from Vtuhr.org: https://vtuhr.org/articles/10.21061/vtuhr.v3i0.21.

Smith, S. S. (2015, August 18). Gustavus Adolphus Revolutionized European Warfare. Retrieved from Investors.com: https://www.investors.com/news/management/leaders-and-success/gustavus-adolphus-father-of-modern-warfare/.

Sorkin, A. D. (2015, September 11). How to Finance an Emperor's Election. Retrieved from The New Yorker: https://www.newyorker.com/news/amy-davidson/how-to-finance-an-emperors-election.

Study.com. (2023, October 30). The Dual Monarchy of Austria-Hungary. Retrieved from Study.com: https://study.com/learn/lesson/hungarian-austrian-dual-monarchy-ausgleich.html#:~:text=The%20Ausgleich%2C%20or%20the%20formal,Ferenc%20Deak%2C%20and%20other%20delegates.

Sun, L. (2020, Fall). Late Imperial China, Silver, and Global Trade Routes. Retrieved from Association for Asian Studies: https://www.asianstudies.org/publications/eaa/archives/late-imperial-china-silver-and-global-trade-routes/.

The Art Story. (20232, October 31). Summary of the Vienna Secession. Retrieved from Theartsotry.org: https://www.theartstory.org/movement/vienna-secession/.

The Art Story. (2023, October 25). Diego Velazquez. Retrieved from Theartstory.org: https://www.theartstory.org/artist/velazquez-diego/.

The Bohemian Religious Peace (July 1609). (2023, October 28). Retrieved from GHDI: https://ghdi.ghi-dc.org/sub_document.cfm?document_id=4501.

The Economist. (2016, December 24). How Vienna Produced Ideas That Shaped the West. Retrieved from Economist.com: https://www.economist.com/christmas-specials/2016/12/24/how-vienna-produced-ideas-that-shaped-the-west.

The Museum of Fine Arts, Houston. (2023, October 25). "Habsburg Splendor: Masterpieces from Vienna's Imperial Collections". Retrieved from MFAH.org: https://www.mfah.org/press/major-traveling-exhibition-masterpieces-austrian-habsburg-dynasty-brings.

The Royal Hampshire Regiment. (2023, October 28). The War of the Spanish Succession. Retrieved from Royalhampshirereiment.org: https://www.royalhampshireregiment.org/about-the-museum/timeline/war-spanish-succession/.

The World of the Habsburgs. (2023, October 21). Rudolf I of Habsburgs: From "Poor Count" to King of the Romans. Retrieved from The World of the Habsburgs: https://www.habsburger.net/en/chapter/rudolf-i-habsburg-poor-count-king-romans.

The World of the Habsburgs. (2023, October 21). The Habsburgs' Origins as a Swiss Noble Family. Retrieved from The World of the Habsburgs: https://www.habsburger.net/en/chapter/habsburgs-origins-swiss-noble-family.

Visiting Vienna. (2023, June 7). Prince Eugene: What You Need to Know. Retrieved from Visitingvienna.com: https://www.visitingvienna.com/culture/prince-eugene-savoy/.

Wethey, H. E. (2023, September 23). El Greco. Retrieved from Britannica.com: https://www.britannica.com/biography/El-Greco.

Wilson, D. (2020, May 23). The 1618 Defenestration of Prague Explained. Retrieved from History Extra: https://www.historyextra.com/period/stuart/1618-defenestration-prague-facts-history-explained-what-happened-why-castle-protestant-catholic/.

Woods, A. (2005, July 19). The 400th Anniversary of Don Quixote: Spain in the Age of Cervantes. Retrieved from Marxist.com: https://www.marxist.com/don-quixote-cervantes150705.htm.

Printed in Great Britain
by Amazon

54280792R00077